NATIVE NORTH AMERICAN ALMANAC

NATIVE NORTH AMERICAN ALMANAC

Volume 2

Cynthia Rose and Duane Champagne, Editors

An Imprint of Gale Research Inc.

NATIVE NORTH AMERICAN ALMANAC

Cynthia Rose and Duane Champagne, *Editors*

Staff

Sonia Benson, *U·X·L Associate Developmental Editor*
Thomas L. Romig, *U·X·L Publisher*

Keith Reed, *Permissions Associate (Pictures)*
Margaret A. Chamberlain, *Permissions Supervisor (Pictures)*

Mary Kelley, *Production Associate*
Evi Seoud, *Assistant Production Manager*
Mary Beth Trimper, *Production Director*

Mary Krzewinski, *Cover Designer*
Cynthia Baldwin, *Art Director*

The Graphix Group, *Typesetter*

 ™ This book is printed on acid-free paper that meets the minimum requirements of American National Standard for Information Sciences—Permanence Paper for Printed Library Materials, ANSI Z39.48-1984.

ISBN 0-8103-9820-6 (Set)
ISBN 0-8103-9814-1 (Volume 1)
ISBN 0-8103-9815-X (Volume 2)

Printed in the United States of America

Published simultaneously in the United Kingdom
by Gale Research International Limited
(An affiliated company of Gale Research Inc.)

I(T)P™

The trademark **ITP** is used under license.

READER'S GUIDE

Native North American Almanac features a comprehensive range of historical and current information on the life and culture of the Native peoples of the United States and Canada. Organized into 24 subject chapters, including major culture areas, activism, and religion, the volumes contain more than two hundred black-and-white photographs and maps, a glossary of terms used throughout the text, and a cumulative subject index.

Related reference sources:

Native North American Biography profiles 135 Native Americans, both living and deceased, prominent in their fields, ranging from civil rights to athletics, politics to literature, entertainment to science, religion to the military. A black-and-white portrait accompanies each entry, and a cumulative subject index lists all individuals by field of endeavor.

Native North American Chronology explores significant social, political, economic, cultural, and educational milestones in the history of the Native peoples of the United States and Canada. Arranged by year and then by month and day, the chronology spans from prehistory to modern times and contains more than 70 illustrations, extensive cross references, and a cumulative subject index.

Native North American Voices presents full or excerpted speeches, sermons, orations, poems, testimony, and other notable spoken works of Native Americans. Each entry is accompanied by an introduction and boxes explaining terms and events to which the speech alludes, as well as several pertinent illustrations.

Advisors

Special thanks are due for the invaluable comments and suggestions provided by U·X·L's Native North American books advisors:

Naomi Caldwell-Wood
President, American Indian
 Library Association

Victoria Gale
Librarian, Lodge Grass High School
Lodge Grass, Montana

Comments and Suggestions

We welcome your comments on *Native North American Almanac* as well as your suggestions for topics to be featured in future editions. Please write: Editors, *Native North American Almanac,* U·X·L, 835 Penobscot Bldg., Detroit, Michigan 48226-4094; call toll-free: 1-800-877-4253; or fax: 313-961-6348.

A NOTE ON TERMINOLOGY: IS *INDIAN* THE RIGHT NAME?

Throughout the *Native North American Almanac* a variety of terms are used for Native North Americans, such as *Indian, American Indian, Native, aboriginal,* and *First Nations.* The Native peoples of the Americas have the unfortunate distinction of having been given the wrong name by the Europeans who first arrived on the continent, mistakenly thinking they had arrived in India. The search for a single name, however, has not been entirely successful. In the United States, *Native American* has been used but has recently fallen out of favor with some groups, and *American Indian* is now preferred by some groups.

Canadians, too, have wrestled with this question of names, and many Native Canadians reject the appellation of *Indian*. Métis and Inuit in Canada will not answer to the name *Indian*. Similarly, in Alaska the Inuit, Yupik, and Aleut peoples consider themselves distinct from Indian peoples and do not wish to be called *Indian*. The Canadians have developed a range of terms such as *Native, aboriginal, First Nations,* and *First Peoples,* which in many ways more accurately describes the Native peoples.

Native peoples in North America do not form a single ethnic group and are better understood as thousands of distinct communities and cultures. Many Native peoples have distinct languages, religious beliefs, ceremonies, and social and political systems. No one word can characterize such diversity. The inclusive word *Indian* denotes the collection of people who occupied the North American continent, but it says little about the diversity and independence of the cultures.

The best way to characterize Native North Americans is by recognizing their specific tribal or community identities, such as Blackfeet, Cherokee, or Cree. Such identifications more accurately capture the unique and varied tribal and cultural distinctions found among Native North American peoples.

In compiling this book, every effort has been made to keep Native tribal and comunity identities distinct, but, by necessity, inclusive terminology is often used. We do not wish to offend anyone, but rather than favor one term for Native North American people, the editors have used a variety of terminology, trying always to use the most appropriate term in the particular context.

CONTENTS

Volume 1

Volume 2

PICTURE CREDITS

Cover art is based on photograph, appearing on page 307, of the American Indian Dance Theatre performing an Eagle Dance. Courtesy of Hanay Geiogamah.

The photographs and illustrations appearing in *Native North American Almanac* were received from the following sources:

Courtesy of Jesse D. Jennings: p. 4; **courtesy of Tessa Macintosh, NT government:** pp. 6, 92, 134, 135, 139, 193, 226, 252, 256, 281, 290; **National Museum of Natural History, Department of Anthropology, Smithsonian Insititution:** p. 8 (catalogue number 317614), p. 293 (catalogue number 323868); **courtesy of American Heritage Press:** pp. 12, 89, 155, 182, 189, 205, 207; **courtesy of Mark Nohl, NM Economics & Tourism Dept., Joseph M. Montoya Building, 100 St. Francis Drive, Santa Fe, NM 87503:** pp. 13, 195; **courtesy of the National Archives of Canada:** p. 20, 142 (C18084); **courtesy of Utah State Historical Society:** p. 23; **Duane Champagne:** pp. 24, 97; **courtesy of Denver Public Library, Western History Department:** pp. 28, 163, 223; **courtesy of Imre Sutton:** p. 31; **courtesy of the Government Printing Office, Washington, D.C.:** p. 37; **courtesy of the Minnesota Historical Society:** pp. 40, 219; **courtesy of the National Library of Canada, Rare Book Collection/Bibliotheque Nationale du Canada, Collection des livres rares:** p. 41; **drawing by John Kahionhes Fadden:** p. 43; **courtesy of the Buffalo and Erie County Historical Society:** pp. 45, 326; **courtesy of Daniel Rogers:** p. 56; **courtesy of Paul Natonabah,** *Navajo Times:* pp. 59, 101, 165, 187, 215, 217, 218, 221, 269; **courtesy of Owen Seumptewa:** pp. 62, 63, 286; **courtesy of Royal Ontario Museum, Toronto, Ontario, Canada:** p. 68, 123, 142; **courtesy of Ken Blackbird:** pp. 73, 74; **courtesy of John Webber, artist, Special Collections Division, University of Washington Libraries, Negative N. NA 3918:** p. 80; **courtesy of Stephen Lehmer:** pp. 83, 84, 96, 152, 181, 277, 329, 330; **photo by Oklahoma Tourism:** p. 98; **courtesy of the Nevada State Historical Society:** p. 102; **courtesy of Historic Resource Department, Riverside, CA:** p. 110; **courtesy of Diego Romero:** p. 111; **courtesy of Los Angeles City Library:** pp. 112, 113, 115; **courtesy of Glenda Ahhaitty: p. 147; courtesy of Anthropological Archives, Smithsonian:** p.

WORDS TO KNOW

A

aboriginal: native; the first or earliest group living in a particular area. When a group of people is called *aboriginal* it is generally being defined in contrast to colonizers or invaders of the land the group occupies. In Canada in the 1990s, the term *aboriginal* is commonly used to describe Native peoples.

aboriginal rights: privileges or claims that aboriginal people have, based on the fact that their ancestors were first to live in an area. Some examples of *aboriginal rights* are ownership of the land and its resources, the right to self-government, and the freedom to choose beliefs and cultural practices.

aboriginal title: the claim of the first inhabitants of an area to title or legal ownership of that area, based on the fact that they lived there first.

adjudicated: decided by a judgment, usually by a court of law.

AFN: See Assembly of First Nations

AIM: See American Indian Movement.

Alaska Native Claims Settlement Act (ANCSA): an act of Congress passed in 1971 that gave Alaska Natives 44 million acres of land and $962.5 million. In exchange, Alaska Natives gave up all claim to other lands in Alaska.

alienation: a feeling of being separated or withdrawn from society, from one's own identity, or from one's roots.

allotment: the practice of dividing up Indian reservations into privately owned parcels (pieces) of land. Tribes traditionally owned their lands in common, meaning that the tribe owned the land and all members could use and enjoy it. *Allotting* lands disrupted Indian societies greatly.

American Indian Movement (AIM): an activist organization founded by Native Americans in Minneapolis, Minnesota, during the 1960s.

annuities: money paid yearly to American Indians, according to the terms of treaties or agreements to give up lands. The U.S. government paid out *annuities* because it preferred to spread out the cost of payments over a period of years, rather than having to pay the money all at once.

ANCSA: See Alaska Native Claims Settlement Act.

archaeology: the study of prehistory; a scientific process of digging up and examining fossil relics, artifacts, and monuments of past human life.

Articles of Confederation: the original agreement made by the thirteen colonies in 1777 when they decided to form a new and independent country.

artifact: any item made by humans, such as tools or weapons, which is found by archaeologists or others who seek clues to the past.

Assembly of First Nations (AFN): the national organization that represents Indian nations to the Canadian government.

assimilate: to become like the dominant society (those in power, or in the majority).

B

band: Canadian term that originally meant a social and economic group of nomadic hunting peoples. Since Canada's confederation, however, the term also means any community of Indians registered under the Indian Act.

band council: in Canada, a form of Native government made up of a chief and council members who are responsible for conducting the band's business.

Berengia: the land bridge that existed over 15,000 years ago between present-day Siberia and Alaska.

BIA: See Bureau of Indian Affairs.

bilingual: speaking two languages fluently.

boarding school: a school where students live all or part of the year.

Bosque Redondo: the Navajo reservation in present-day New Mexico where the Navajo were forced to live between 1864 and 1868.

broadcast: to make public through radio or television.

Bureau of Indian Affairs (BIA): the U.S. government agency that oversees tribal lands, education, and other aspects of Indian life.

C

capitalism: a type of economy in which property and businesses are owned by individuals or group of individuals (rather than being owned by the government or by the society as a whole). Profits in a *capitalist* economy are based on competition and enrich the individual owner. Workers are paid a wage, or an agreed-upon amount, for their efforts.

census: an official count of the people in an area. A *census* is usually taken by the government, and includes information such as the number of people living in a house or apartment, their age, sex, occupation, and other facts.

ceremony: a special act or set of acts, performed by members of a group on special occasions, usually structured by the group's set of conventions and beliefs.

CERT: See Council of Energy Resource Tribes.

Civilized Tribes: See Five Civilized Tribes.

clan: a group of related families, which forms the basic social unit for some Indian societies.

comprehensive claim: in Canada, a land claim based on aboriginal rights to the land, where no treaties are involved.

collective good: the well-being of the group as a whole, usually resulting from the members working together cooperatively.

confederacy: a group of people, states, or nations joined together for a special purpose or mutual support.

conservation: protection and preservation of something; a carefully planned management system to prevent exploitation, destruction, or overuse.

conservative: traditional; wishing to preserve what is already established, such as traditions or political and economic structures.

convert: to cause a person or group to change their religious beliefs. A *convert* is a person who has been *converted* to a new belief.

cooperative: a type of business in which members share in the profits and losses; sometimes called a co-op. As the name implies, *cooperatives* are based on the cooperation of members; they aim to increase the wealth of the whole group, not just certain individuals.

Council of Energy Resource Tribes (CERT): an organization formed by tribes in the United States for the purpose of managing the natural resources on their reservations.

creation stories: sacred myths or stories that explain how the earth and its beings were created.

culture: the set of beliefs, social habits, and ways of surviving in the environment that are held by a particular social group. *Culture* is also the word for a group that shares these traits.

culture area: a region in which several tribes live and share similar cultures; their languages may or may not be similar.

curriculum: the courses or classes offered in a school.

D

Dawes General Allotment Act of 1887: a law that supported the U.S. government's practice of dividing up reservation lands into small parcels, which were given to individual tribe members.

demography: the study of populations, including information on migration, birth, death, health, and marriage.

displace; displacement: to remove a group from its usual place of residence.

diversity: variety; difference.

division of labor: dividing up, or sharing, different kinds of work among the people of a society.

drums: groups of Indian men singers (and recently women singers, too) often from different tribes, who get together to perform at powwows or other gatherings.

E

economy: the way a group obtains, produces, and distributes the goods it needs; the way it supports itself and accumulates its wealth.

economic development: the process of creating or improving a society's economy.

epidemic: the rapid spread of a disease so that many people in an area have it at the same time.

extinct: no longer existing. Many Indian tribes became *extinct* due to diseases brought by European explorers and settlers. Languages can become *extinct* when no one remains alive to remember or speak them, and they have not been written down.

F

First Nations: a term used for aboriginal peoples. The term *First Nations* began to be used in Canada in the 1970s.

Five Civilized Tribes: a name given to the Cherokee, Choctaw, Chickasaw, Creek, and Seminole during the mid-1800s. These tribes were so named because they had democratic governments, wrote constitutions, and ran schools in which the students could often read and write better than white children living nearby.

formal education: structured learning that takes place in a school or college, under the supervision of teachers.

G

gender role: the expectation within a social group of particular functions and behaviors from a person, based on whether that person is a male or a female.

general assistance: help, usually in the form of money, given by the government to people who are unable to support themselves.

Ghost Dance: a revitalization (renewal or rebirth) movement that arose in the 1870s. The *Ghost Dance* movement aimed to bring back to life traditional lifestyles, the buffalo, and many of the people killed by epidemic diseases.

Great Basin: an elevated region in the western United States in which all water drains toward the center. The *Great Basin* covers part of Nevada, California, Colorado, Utah, Oregon, and Wyoming.

guardian spirit: a sacred power, usually embodied in an animal such as a hawk, deer, or turtle, that reveals itself to an individual, offering help in important matters such as hunting or healing the sick.

H

harmony: a condition in which feelings, ideas, and actions all work together smoothly, or a state in which people work together in concert; the idea comes from music, when several notes played at the same time seem to fit together to make up one sound that is pleasing.

Haudenosaunee: the name of the people often called Iroquois or Five Nations. *Haudenosaunee* means "People of the Longhouse."

higher education: education at a college, university, or other post-secondary learning institution.

holistic: concerned with all the aspects of health, including the physical, mental, emotional, and spiritual. *Holistic* medicine heals the whole person—body, mind, and spirit.

I

image: in art, a picture or representation of something; for example, a warrior might dream of an eagle and then draw an *image* of the eagle on his teepee. In a social context an *image* is a mental picture or idea of someone or something held by a person or group. When Hollywood movies repeatedly portray Indians in a particular way, the American public may form an inaccurate *image* of what American Indians are like.

immunity: resistance to disease; the ability to be exposed to disease without necessarily getting it.

Indian Act: in Canada, the law that defines government policies toward Indians, first passed in 1876 and revised in 1985.

Indian country: reservations and sometimes nearby lands where Indian government and customs rule.

Indian Reorganization Act of 1934 (IRA): a law that ended allotment and gave tribes the option to form their own governments.

Indian Territory: the area of present-day Kansas and Oklahoma where the U.S. government once planned to move all Indians. In 1880, nearly one-third of all U.S. Indians lived there.

indigenous: native to an area.

informal education: learning that takes place outside of a school or classroom. Learning—through observation, participation, or practice—things like how to prepare for a ceremony, make a teepee, or speak a language.

interior: the part of a country or region that is away from the coast or border; inland.

Inuit: those aboriginal peoples who live north of the treeline in Alaska, Canada, and Greenland. The *Inuit* were formerly known as Eskimos. The word *Inuit* means people.

Inuk: singular form of Inuit.

IRA: See Indian Reorganization Act.

Iroquois Confederacy: an alliance formed by the Mohawk, Cayuga, Onondaga, Oneida, and Seneca, and later joined by the Tuscarora; also called League of the Iroquois, Five Nations, or Six Nations (after the Tuscarora joined).

K

Kachina: a group of spirits among the Pueblo; also refers to dolls made in the image of *Kachina* spirits.

kiva: among the Pueblo, a circular underground room used for ceremonies.

L

land runs: during the 1890s, spectacular one-day chances for non-Natives to get former Indian lands in Oklahoma .

language family: a group of languages that are different from one another but are related. These languages share similar words, sounds, or word structures. The languages are similar either because they have borrowed words from each other or because they originally came from the same *parent language.*

legal system: a group's laws, and the way they are learned and enforced.

legend: a story or folktale that tells about people or events in the distant past and is believed by many people.

life expectancy: the average number of years a person may expect to live.

literacy: the state of being able to read and write.

loan words: words that people who speak one language have taken or "borrowed" from another language.

Long Walk of the Navajo: the enforced 300-mile walk of the Navajo to Bosque Redondo in 1864.

longhouse: a large, long building in which several families live together; usually found among Northwest Coast and Iroquois peoples.

M

maize: corn. Maize was first grown in Mexico over 6,000 years ago.

Manifest Destiny: the belief held by many Americans during the 1840s that the United States should expand across the continent, and that fate determined that it should do so.

matrilineal: tracing family relations through the mother; in a *matrilineal* society, names and inheritances are passed down through the mother's side of the family.

media: sources, such as television, radio, theater, films, newspapers, magazines, and other printed matter, through which information, entertainment, and other popular forms of mass communication reach audiences.

Medicine Chest Clause: in Canada, a section of Treaty No. 6 (1876) which promised that the government would provide medical supplies to the Indians.

mercantile: having to do with trade or merchants (people who buy and sell in order to make a profit).

Métis: French word for "mixed-blood." This term has been used in different ways. Usually it refers to a specific group of people in western Canada. The Canadian Constitution recognizes *Métis* as aboriginal peoples. The term is also applied to any people descended from marriages between Europeans and Indians.

migration: movement from one place to another. The *migrations* of Native peoples were often done by the group, with whole nations moving from one area to another.

mission: an organized effort by a religious group to spread its beliefs in other parts of the world; *mission* refers either to the project of spreading a belief system or to the building(s) in which this takes place.

mission school: a school established by missionaries to teach people new religious beliefs, as well as other subjects.

myth: a story passed down through generations, often involving supernatural beings. *Myths* often express religious beliefs or the values of a people. They may attempt to explain how the earth and its beings were created, or why things are as they are.

N

neophyte: a new convert.

nomadic: traveling and relocating often, usually in search of food and other resources or a better climate.

non-recognized tribe: an Indian community that does not have official status with the U.S. government. Such a tribe may have been terminated by the government, or it may never have signed a treaty with the government.

non-status Indians: aboriginal people in Canada whom the government does not recognize officially as Indians under the Indian Act.

non-treaty Indians: aboriginal people whose status with the Canadian government does not involve any treaties.

Nunavut: a proposed new territory covering most of Canada north of the treeline, inhabited primarily by Inuit.

O

open access: a European concept of land use in the sixteenth and seventeenth centuries in which it was held that any area not legally owned by an individual or other legal party could be used for hunting or obtaining other resources without regard to traditional territorial control.

oral traditions: history, mythology, folklore, and other foundations of a culture that have been passed by spoken word, often in the form of stories, from generation to generation within a culture group.

oral literature: oral traditions that are written down after enjoying a long life in spoken form among a people.

P

pan-Indian, pan-tribal: taking into account all Indians regardless of tribes; *pan-Indian* groups often organize Native peoples from many tribes to work on issues that affect all Indians.

parent language: a language that is the common source of two or more languages that came into being at a later time.

passive resistance: going against a power or authority by means of not cooperating with them.

perspective: the viewpoint from which something is seen; the background or position from which a subject is mentally viewed or considered.

petroglyph: a carving or engraving on rock; a common form of ancient art.

peyote: a substance obtained from the button-like parts of the mescal cactus plant that some Indian groups use as part of their religious practices. By eating these buttons, which stimulate the nervous system, perceptions can be enhanced or altered during a ceremony.

pictograph: a simple picture representing a historical event.

policy: a statement in which a government tells how it will handle certain situations or people, or what its goals are.

population density: the number of people living in a given unit of area. The *population density* of New York City is very high because a lot of people live there in a small area. In contrast, the Mojave desert has a low *population density.*

potlatch: a feast or ceremony, commonly held among Northwest Coast groups; also called "giveaways." During a *potlatch,* goods are given away to show the host's generosity and wealth. Potlatches celebrate major life events such as birth, death, or marriage.

prehistory: a period of time in a given area when writing did not exist and there are therefore no written records to document the history of the era.

province: a district or division of a country. Canada is divided into ten *provinces* and two territories.

pueblo, Pueblo: pueblos are the many-storied stone or adobe Indian villages of the American Southwest. *Pueblo* is also the name that has been given to the Indian people who live in these villages.

R

rancheria: a small Indian reservation, usually in California.

ratify: to approve or confirm. In the United States, the Senate *ratified* treaties with the Indians.

Red Power: A term used to describe the Native American activism movement of the 1960s, in which people from many tribes came together to protest the injustices of American policies toward Native Americans.

Removal Act: an act passed by Congress in 1830 which directed that all Indians should be moved to Indian Territory, west of the Mississippi River.

Removal Period: the time, mostly between 1830 and 1860, when most Indians were removed from their homelands and relocated west of the Mississippi.

reservation: land set aside by the U.S. government for the use of groups of Indians.

reserve: In Canada, land set aside for specific Indian bands. *Reserve* means in Canada approximately what *reservation* means in the United States.

revitalization: the feeling or movement in which something seems to come back to life after having been quiet or inactive for a period of time.

ritual: a formal act that is performed in basically the same way each time; the acts that are performed in a ceremony or part of a ceremony.

rural: having to do with the country; opposite of urban.

S

sacrilege: the violation of what is sacred to a group.

self-determination: often means a person's right to choose his or her own way of life. The term also refers to the right of a group of people to choose and direct the way of life within their community, including the authority to make and enforce laws.

shaman: a person within certain Native American groups who understands supernatural matters. *Shamans* traditionally performed in rituals and were expected to cure the sick, envision the future, and help with hunting and other economic activities.

sister languages: languages that stem from a common source, the *parent language*. *Sister languages* usually differ from each other because they developed in a different area, but they retain some or many similarities.

smallpox: a very contagious disease which spread across North America and killed many thousands of Indians. Survivors had skin that was badly scarred.

sovereignty: self-rule; freedom from the rule or control of outside parties.

specific claim: in Canada, a claim by aboriginals based on rights given by treaty or legislation.

status Indians: in Canada, those aboriginals who meet the definition of Indian as determined by the Indian Act.

subsistence economy: a way of keeping alive by producing food and other goods for one's own use. In a *subsistence economy,* people may grow their own fruits and vegetables, raise livestock or hunt, and make their own clothing. *Subsistence* farmers use what they grow rather than selling it.

Sun Dance: a renewal and purification (cleansing) ceremony, performed among many Plains Indians such as the Sioux and Cheyenne.

sweat lodge: a sacred ceremony often conducted by a medicine man. A small dome-shaped lodge is built, and steam is created by pouring water on hot rocks. The *sweat lodge* is used for a variety of purposes, including spiritual healing.

sweetgrass ceremony: a ceremony in which sweetgrass is burned and participants rub the smoke on themselves—similar to the use of incense in other religions.

syllabary: a system of writing that uses characters (letters) to represent whole syllables (rather than letters representing consonants and vowels, as in an alphabet system).

symbol, symbolic meaning: a *symbol* is something that stands for or represents an idea, emotion, or any other concept; for example, to some cultures the eagle is a *symbol* of power and strength. A *symbolic meaning* is the idea that the symbol represents; for example, the *symbolic meaning* of the eagle is power and strength.

T

termination: the policy of the U.S. government during the 1950s and 1960s to end its trust relationship with Indian nations.

title: a statement or document that shows ownership of a piece of property. In the United States and Canada, one must have *title* to a piece of property in order to be recognized as the legal owner.

totem: an animal, bird, fish, plant, or other natural

object that a person or group takes as its emblem or protective spirit.

Trail of Tears: a series of forced marches in the 1830s caused by the U.S. government's removal policy. Cherokee, Creek, Seminole, and perhaps some Choctaw were moved from the Southeast to Indian Territory, causing the deaths of thousands.

travois: a hauling vehicle made of two long poles that bear a platform or net to carry loads. Before the Spanish brought horses to North America, many Native groups used dogs to pull the *travois*.

treaty: an agreement between two parties or two nations, signed by both, usually defining the benefits to both parties that will result from one side giving up title to a territory of land.

treaty Indians: in Canada, those Indians who are entitled to benefits under treaties signed between 1725 and 1921.

tribe: a group of Natives who share a name, language, culture, and ancestors; in Canada, called a band.

tribalism: loyalty to one's group.

Trickster: a common culture hero in Indian myth and legend. *Trickster* takes different forms among various groups; for example, Coyote in the Southwest, Ikhtomi Spider in the High Plains, and Jay or Wolverine in Canada.

trust: a relationship between two parties (or groups), in which one is responsible for acting in the other's best interests. The U.S. government has a *trust* relationship with tribal nations. Many tribes do not own their lands outright; according to treaty, the government owns the land "in trust" and tribes are given the use of it.

tundra: plains in arctic and subarctic regions that consist of a mucky soil on top of a permanently frozen subsoil. Plant life in the *tundra* is usually limited to mosses, lichen, and small shrubs.

U

unemployment rate: the percent of the population that is looking for work, but unable to find any. People who have quit looking for work are not included in *unemployment* figures.

urban: having to do with cities and towns.

urbanization: the process of moving from a rural to an urban environment, or from the country to the city. For many Native Americans, *urbanization* means moving from the reservation to a city or town.

V

values: the ideals that a community of people shares.

vision quest: a sacred ceremony in which a person (often a teenage boy) goes off alone and fasts, living without food or water for a period of days. During that time, he hopes to learn about his spiritual side and to have a vision of a guardian spirit who will give him help and strength.

visual arts: art forms that aim to please solely through the eye, as opposed to dramatic arts or literature, which also involve reading or listening. Examples of visual arts are painting, photography, sculpture, textiles, and pottery.

W

wampum: small cylinder-shaped beads cut from the shell of the quahog (a large clam found on the Atlantic coast). Long strings of *wampum* were used as money.

wampum belt: a broad woven belt of wampum, used to record history, treaties among the tribes, or treaties with colonists or governments.

weir: a barricade used to funnel fish toward people who wait to catch them.

NATIVE NORTH AMERICAN ALMANAC

15
Religion

FACT FOCUS

- In Native American cultures, almost every activity and aspect of life has sacred meaning.
- Not one of the 250 Native American languages spoken today has a separate word for religion.
- The Native American Church is the largest and fastest-growing Indian religion in North America today.
- The Native American Church and many other Native American religions that have arisen since Europeans arrived in North America combine Christian teachings with traditional Indian beliefs and practices.

What Is Religion for Native Americans?

In most Native American cultures, religion is not something separate from everyday life. Religion is woven into the very fabric of life, and it is impossible to say where religion ends and the rest of life begins. In most traditional American Indian cultures, **sacred** (or religious) meaning can be found in almost every activity and aspect of life. House building, hunting, gathering, farming, mining, medicine and healing, eating, sleeping and dreams, fire-making, toolmaking, art, music, storytelling, time—all have sacred meaning in Native American cultures. Thus, these activities traditionally involve prayer or **ritual**.

Among the 250 Native American languages spoken today, not one has a word for "religion." Since religion is not a separate aspect of life for most Native American peoples, it is an assumed basis of all words.

Native American Religious Beliefs

All Things Are Related

From the beginning, most Native American religious beliefs and practices have grown out of both a respect for nature and an understanding that the world is a dangerous place. Most Native American religions do not separate spiritual and physical beings as Christian traditions do; spirits exist within the physical world of animals, plants, and human beings. These spiritual beings of the world can either help or harm people. Native peoples try to ensure safety and success and avoid harm by showing their respect for nature and the spirit world through rituals and **ceremonies.** And for much the same reason, they try to maintain a respectful and caring relationship with fellow human beings.

Many Native American religions center around a profound understanding that all things in the world are related—people, sky, earth, rivers, animals, plants, spirits, moon and stars. Because all things are related, a change or action by one individual being will affect things in the world. Thus, all beings and powers depend on each other. This is the meaning of "interdependence" for Native American peoples.

Many Native peoples hold the belief that an individual's—or a group's—actions can cause either success or disaster. If they conduct their lives and ceremonies properly, good fortune will result; if they do not, misfortune and suffering will almost certainly occur. In spite of the many differences among the tribes of North America, they all share this ancient religious belief.

Most of the major tribal rituals—the Green Corn ceremony, the Sun Dance, and the Medicine Society ceremonies—celebrate the interdependence of humans and the great beings of the universe. The great beings and powers depend on humans as well—it is not a one-way street!

When the Lakota and other Plains peoples call upon the Great Spirit, they also address many other beings as "all my relatives." These beings or relatives are sometimes called "grandmother" and "grandfather." In this way many Native cultures express their desire to have a caring relationship with all beings and forces in the universe.

A ZUNI MYTH: THE KACHINAS

The mythology of the Zuni of New Mexico describes a time when human beings and the Kachinas (ancestral spirit beings) competed with each other over ownership of the deer and other game. After a prolonged battle in which humans and Kachinas found themselves equally powerful, humans decided to use trickery to win the contest. Rather than sharing the deer with the Kachinas, which would promote balance, humans imprisoned all the game in a place that the Kachinas could not find. The conflict ended when the Kachinas acknowledged human ownership of the deer and, in return, humans recognized that the Kachinas had control of corn and other seeds. This resolution showed the uselessness of conflict. Each group desired the resources of the other; interdependence and a positive system of give-and-take between the human and the spirit world were necessary and rewarding.

Balance and Harmony

Native American cultures tend to value balance and harmony in all aspects of life. They strive to create a sense of beauty, harmony, and well-being in their rituals and ceremonies. All Native peoples have histor-

Sun Dance at Pine Ridge, a Sioux reservation in southern South Dakota.

ically believed that they must seek the proper balance in their relations with each other and with the rest of the world. Power and responsibility must be shared.

Native Americans often celebrated their encounters with strangers by sharing a peace pipe, or conducting ceremonies in which tobacco (a sacred plant) was burned. These rituals, conducted with both friends and enemies, were intended to affirm the relatedness of all living things. Today these rituals often take the form of talking circles, in which Indians from once-hostile tribes seek to understand each other better. The act of seeking peace and harmony with nature and fellow human beings is the very heart of traditional Indian religion.

The Importance of the Collective Good

Whether large or small societies, hunters or farmers, living in the icy north or the desert south—all Native cultures are based on a belief that the well-being of the whole group is more important than the wishes of any one individual. In other words, Native peoples believe that the **collective good** (the good of the group) is primary. This belief is in stark contrast to the Western traditions of competition, rugged individualism, and self-interest.

The belief in putting the well-being of the group first probably grew out of the realities of everyday life in Native North America. Hunting peoples, for example, depended for their very lives on kinship and cooperation with each other and with the natural world. In societies in which people faced starvation if group hunting expeditions were unsuccessful, the luxury of self-interest or individual gain was unthinkable. All were expected

Ceremonies at the death of a chief or of priests. Drawing by Le Moyne, engraving from Theodore de Bry, *America,* Part II, 1591.

to contribute to the group's well-being. Young boys gave their first kill to elders, who thanked them for their skill and gifts. Young girls learned the importance of service from their mothers, aunts, and grandmothers. Unmarried men gave their game to headmen, who distributed food and other goods to those in need. No one—whether young or old, married or unmarried, sickly or healthy—went without food, clothing, and shelter. Attention to the needs of others was the way to gain respect; giving generously was a hallmark of "chiefly" status.

Tribal peoples often isolated individuals whose behavior went against the well-being of the group, using laughter and gossip to correct them. When the group turned their backs on a wayward person, he or she felt the pain of isolation and soon mended his or her ways to comply with the group. Self-interest was tolerated only when it did not interfere with the tribe's well-being. When one person's behavior upset the balance of the group, the group set about to restore balance and harmony.

Celebrations of the Life Cycle

Throughout North America, Indian peoples give thanks to the plants and animals that feed, clothe, and sometimes shelter them and to the herbs that cure and purify them. Many Native American traditions promote treating animal bones with respect, because each being in the world is part of a cycle. The spirits of respectfully treated animals will be reborn and replenish the earth. Indian peoples understand that this cycle of life depends on human action. Humans play an important role in the cosmic cycle of birth, growth, death, and rebirth.

For example, in the Pacific Northwest, the first-catch ceremony has traditionally celebrated the gift of salmon. The first fish of the year was placed on evergreen bows (symbols of enduring life because they stay green all year). People thanked the salmon for being willing to sacrifice its life so that humans can live. Then the salmon was carefully cooked, and each person in the village ate part of this special fish. Finally, the salmon's bones were returned to the water so they would live again.

Similarly, first-fruit ceremonies—honoring the plants that gave food and life to humans—have celebrated the cycles of life all across North America. In the East, the Green Corn ceremony—a purification ritual and an annual celebration of the new year—was widespread. Honors and thanks were given to the corn for giving life to people. The Iroquois have had a variety of rituals, like the "Thanks to the Maple" and the Strawberry festivals. In these ceremonies the people sang and danced to express their gratitude to maple trees and strawberries for their part in supporting the lives of humans.

After the 1750s, when horses became common on the Great Plains, the well-being

WORDS TO KNOW

ceremony: a special act or set of acts, performed by members of a group on special occasions, usually structured by the group's set of conventions and beliefs.

collective good: the well-being of the group as a whole, usually resulting from the members working together cooperatively.

creation stories: myths or stories that explain how the earth and its beings were created.

guardian spirit: a sacred power, usually embodied in an animal such as a hawk, deer, or turtle, that reveals itself to an individual, offering help in important matters such as healing the sick or hunting.

myth: a traditional tale about the Creator, spirits, or other beings that explains some part of the nature and meaning of the universe and human life.

peyote: a substance obtained from the button-like parts of the mescal cactus plant, that some Indian groups use as part of their religious practices. By eating these buttons, which stimulate the nervous system, perceptions can be enhanced or altered during a ceremony.

ritual: a formal act that is performed in basically the same way each time; the acts that are performed in a ceremony or part of the ceremony.

of buffalo and horses and success in war became the focus of ceremonies. The Plains

Huron dancing ceremony to cure sickness, from Samuel de Champlain, *Voyages et descouvertures,* Paris, 1620.

Pawnee, southwestern Pueblo, and California peoples (among others) focused their rituals on the cycles of the seasons and stars.

Native American Mythology

The telling of **myths** and stories is one of the main ways that Native American peoples transmit their culture and beliefs. Some groups kept records with sacred symbols carved on wooden sticks or sewn on wampum belts. But for the most part, American Indian peoples used rituals, ceremonies, and storytelling to carry their history and beliefs from one generation to the next.

A myth is a tale about the Creator, spirits, and other beings that represents the nature and meaning of the universe and human life. Mythology expresses the traditional values of the past in a way that listeners can use in the present. Although the events may not have occurred exactly as told, they carry truths and morals that are important aspects of the group's religious system. Myths offer answers to basic questions such as "Where did we come from?" and "Why are things the way they are?" Myths may also explain why people exist on earth, and how they are supposed to relate to the other beings here and in the spirit world.

Creation Myths

Creation stories (stories that explain how the earth and its beings were created) are the cornerstone of mythology in Native American culture, as in most cultures of the world. There are several types of creation myths. Probably the most common of these are the Earth-Diver myth and the Emergence myth.

The Earth-Diver

There are many earth-diver stories throughout Native North American cultures. The details vary among the tribes, but the main idea is usually the same—a creator acts with the cooperation of various birds and animals to form the earth from a chaotic water world. The creator asks the animals to dive deep into the almost bottomless water. There they must seize a tiny bit of mud, which will be used for forming the earth island. This is an act of daring and **self-sacrifice,** since many animals have died in the attempt. In the end, one of the animals succeeds, and the creator expands the bit of earth into the earth island where people and animals live.

In each tribe's version of the earth-diver story, the particular kind of animal that successfully provided the land upon which the earth was founded is highly respected by the people. In the Iroquois version of the earth-diver myth it is the Turtle who generously offers his back to support the land. In fact, among many Indian cultures the earth island is considered to be the Turtle's back. Some tribes even called North America "Turtle Island." Regardless of how the stories vary from tribe to tribe, they express the same basic moral: that cooperation, service, and self-sacrifice bring order to a chaotic and unruly world. These values are prized among the groups and guide their behavior every day.

Emergence Stories

Emergence stories are another type of creation story. They are common among the Pueblo, Navajo, and Apache in the Southwest, and among the Creek in the Southeast. In emergence stories, people climb out from under the earth, where it is dark and cold. Sometimes the planet is too small and spins rapidly, making the people dizzy. Such conditions drive the people upward in search of a better environment. Sometimes the people, as well as animals or insects, are cast out of the lower world because of immoral behavior. They must find their way to the next world in order to survive. Some fly up, while others are carried by tall plants that

WORDS TO KNOW

sacred: holy; having a spiritual or religious meaning.

self-sacrifice: giving up one's own interests or desires or, in extreme cases, giving up one's life; often done for a cause or from a sense of duty.

shaman: a person who understands supernatural matters and performs in rituals. *Shamans* were often expected to cure the sick, envision the future, and help with hunting and other economic activities.

sweat lodge: a sacred Indian ceremony involving the construction of a lodge made of willow saplings bent to form a dome and covered with animal skins, blankets, or canvas tarps. A hole is dug in the middle of the lodge in which hot rocks are placed and water is poured over them. This is often done by a medicine man in a ceremonial way, often accompanied by praying and singing. The ceremony can have many purposes, including spiritual cleansing and healing.

vision quest: a sacred Indian ceremony in which a person, often a teenage boy, goes to a secluded place to fast (go without food or water), usually for a few days, to learn about the spiritual side of himself. Often the aim of the *vision quest* is to have a vision of one's guardian spirit.

reach into the heavens. Once there, they must live with greater order and harmony, or else risk being destroyed by spirit beings who are offended by their poor behavior. Emergence stories teach the need for moral responsibility.

Culture Heroes

In many Native American stories, culture heroes show people how to act powerfully and responsibly, according to the values of the tribe. These heroes are great beings, often resembling earth-divers in their actions and wisdom. Often they change the shape of the earth itself.

For example, the Wabanaki tell of the culture hero, Gluskap. Gluskap created the rivers and streams of the Northeast by killing a selfish frog who hoarded all the world's water. In California, Coyote performed this same task. In the Southeast, the Cherokee say that a powerful bird formed mountains and valleys by lifting and lowering his wings as he inspected the newly formed earth. Similar roles are played by Raven in the Northwest and the Arctic, Rabbit in the Southeast, and Old Man in the Plains.

The actions and deeds of the culture heroes help explain the importance of acting for the well-being of others. Pain and death are believed to result from the wrong actions of the hero. The culture hero stories account for the existence of poverty, illness, suffering, death, the need to labor, the nature of war, and the forced movement of the tribes. Although the stories are usually very funny and entertaining, they recognize human weaknesses and limitations. The culture heroes, often beset by misfortunes, take problems in stride, thus providing examples of how to deal with obstacles.

Culture heroes are great gift givers. In many myths they create people, and then teach them about edible plants and animals and show them how to make tools such as pots, baskets, nets, spears, canoes, and snowshoes. The knowledge and gifts of the heroes help Indian peoples to live in the Arctic frost or the desert heat. Often a culture hero, such as the Raven of the Tlingit traditions, originally bestowed the people with their main ceremonies and social relations.

Sacred Time

In the Western world, time is generally seen as a sequence of new events unfolding one after the other. For many Indian peoples, however, time is a cycle of repeating events. Whatever happens has happened before, and will happen again. As the saying goes: "There is nothing new under the sun."

American Indian cultures recognize the unique events of history, but consider these events to be less important than what happened in the beginning of time. This idea is reflected in the way many Native Americans have traditionally lived their lives. They do not try to do what has never been done before. Rather, they seek to return to their origins and repeat what their ancestors were taught by the sacred powers in the beginning of time. For example, if a Tlingit is asked why he fishes out of the rivers of the Northwest Coast, he is likely to say "because that is the way the ancestors did it." Asked why he performs a healing ritual the same way every time, a Navajo will probably give the same answer.

Sacred Space

In most American Indian cultures, space has a sacred center—a place where the heavens, earth, and the world below are one. This center is a place Native Americans can go to seek complete unity with their world. Many contemporary American Indians still feel a deep sense of reverence for the traditional center of their world.

For the Cheyenne and Sioux, Bear Butte in South Dakota is a sacred center. When members of the Cheyenne and other Plains tribes visit Bear Butte, they fast and meditate in order to acquire a **guardian spirit.** A guardian spirit is a sacred power, usually embodied in an animal such as a hawk, deer, or turtle. This sacred power reveals itself and offers help in important matters such as hunting or healing the sick.

The Pueblo Indians of New Mexico say they emerged into this world through the earth's navel, located at Blue Lake. Blue Lake is a sacred center for some Pueblo, where important ceremonies, which are kept secret from outsiders, are performed. The Pueblo leave prayer offerings at this sacred center in order to renew the world and bring life to the people.

Traditional Ceremonies Today

A quick overview of the major cultural areas of Native North America shows that many American Indian groups still practice a number of the old ceremonies. Some have been adapted or changed. Others remain the same as they were thousands of years ago.

The Southwest. Some well-known examples of traditional Indian ceremonies are found today among the Pueblo, Hopi, and Zuni peoples of Arizona and New Mexico. Primarily corn farmers, these groups' ceremonies have traditionally centered around the growing and harvesting of corn.

In contemporary times, many Indians continue to participate in traditional ceremonies.

The Papago still mark the new year by harvesting the fruit of the saguaro cactus. In July, whole families camp out in the desert to gather this fruit, which is raked off the plant with a stick. The meat is dug out, and the pods are dropped on the ground, face up, as a prayer for rain. Later the people drink fermented cactus syrup at the council house as a prayer that the plants will receive rain to drink.

The Northeast. The Iroquois federation of tribes, consisting of the Seneca, Mohawk, Onondaga, Oneida, Cayuga, and Tuscarora, once lived in longhouses and practiced important healing rituals during the winter.

Iroquois false face dancers performed healing ceremonies for members of the tribe.

They danced with wooden or cornhusk masks to drive away evil spirits and heal illness. Groups of Iroquois now living in upstate New York still practice these rituals.

The Southeast. Most Southeastern Indians were removed to Oklahoma during the 1830s. However, among the Cherokee who remained in the Southeast, some traditional rituals are still practiced. Old hunting dances, such as the raccoon and opossum dances, are performed. Traditional ceremonies, such as the Green Corn ceremony, are being revived. Eastern Cherokee men also continue to play stickball (an early form of lacrosse), which holds sacred meaning. Prior to the game, the men pray to be given the agility of the deer, the good vision of the eagle, and the fury of

the rattlesnake. After playing, the stickball players "go to the water," or bathe in the river in order to be cleansed and purified.

Small groups of Choctaw, Chickasaw, and Creek also remain in the Southeast. Traditional rituals, like the Green Corn ceremony, continue side by side with newer religious ceremonies.

The Great Lakes. The Ojibway of the Great Lakes regions of Canada and the United States continue to practice traditional mid-winter healing rituals. Of all Ojibway curing ceremonies, the Midewewin, or Grand Medicine Society, seems to be the most important. New members who have had a supernatural vision are inducted into the society and taught healing practices by an older member. [Also see Health chapter.]

Another Great Lakes tribe, the Winnebago, continue to perform the traditional Medicine Dance, a four-day ceremony similar to the Ojibway's Grand Medicine Society. The **vision quest** is also very much alive among them. In the vision quest, Winnebago people go into the woods and fast in the hope that their guardian spirit will appear to them in the form of an animal.

The Subarctic. Shamanism is still common in the subarctic regions of Canada. **Shamans** are people who communicate directly with the spirit world by sending their souls out of their bodies during a trance. Shamans are expected to cure the sick, see into the future, and help with hunting and other vital activities.

The Arctic. The Inuit have preserved many traditional rituals. For example, the Inuit of Alaska perform the bladder ceremony to mark the beginning of a new year. In this ceremony the Inuit burn caribou and

R.Holata Outina.

Native leaders often consulted shamans on important issues. Drawing by Le Moyne; engraving from T. de Bry, *America,* part II, 1591.

bird bladders. They also puncture a seal bladder and place it back into the sea, returning the spirit of the dead animal to the master of animals. This is done to ensure that game will be recreated for another year.

The Northwest Coast. On the Northwest Coast the best-known ceremonies involve the harvesting of salmon. For example, northern tribes such as the Tlingit, Tsimshian, and Haida mark each new year with a salmon ritual. They take the first salmon from the rivers and address it with ritual and prayer.

Among the central Northwest Coast tribes such as the Nootka, Chinook, and Kwakiutl

the potlatch ceremony is still practiced. Potlatches occur on important occasions, such as the start of a new year, the building of a new house, a marriage, or a funeral. They involve giving away or burning extra material goods. Potlatches, which increase the social status of the person who gives them, usually mark the end of something old and the beginning of something new.

The Great Basin. For the Paiute and Shoshoni, ceremonies were never very elaborate. The Circle Dance, for example, is a simple dance where everyone holds hands. In California, the Hupa continue to speak their native language and perform their most important ceremonies—the Jumping Dance and the White Deerskin Dance. These ceremonies last several days, and use elaborate costumes and ritual objects. Hupa stories of creation are told during these ceremonies. It is understood that following the ceremonies, the world will be renewed for another year.

The Plains. Plains Indians such as the Sioux and Crow have revived the traditional Sun Dance. In the Sun Dance, small wooden sticks are tied to a pole and placed under the skin of a man's chest. He then looks at the sun and blows an eagle bone whistle until he tears himself free. The Sun Dance started off as a rite of self-sacrifice, to show thanks for some blessing that had been received. Today the Sun Dance seems to be practiced in order to obtain sacred power, similar to the vision quest.

Plains Indians continue to perform the vision quest for guardian spirits. They also participate in the **sweat lodge** ritual. The sweat lodge is a cone-shaped structure in which steam is produced by pouring water on heated rocks. The steam purifies the participants' souls and bodies.

Sacred Hunting

Many rituals are performed before, during, and after the hunt. However, for many Native American cultures hunting is not just an everyday activity surrounded by prayer and ritual. Hunting in itself is a sacred ceremony with religious meaning.

By hunting, men impose their wills on the animal world, which is considered sacred to most Native peoples. A hunter therefore feels some shame for killing an animal. Native Americans throughout North America offer prayers of apology and for-

Sun Dance piercing at Crow Dog's place, 1971.

giveness to the spirits of animals after a successful hunt.

A Sioux Indian was once recorded apologizing to a buffalo for having killed it. He said he killed only because his family needed the meat and skins. The hunter continued to say that when he died his body would become fertilizer for the earth. And on this earth, grasses would grow to feed future generations of buffalo.

Many American Indian groups give thanks to the Chief Animal Spirit for allowing one of its creatures to be slain. They believe it is the will of this spirit to allow animals to sacrifice themselves to the hunter. After the hunter offers thanks he disposes of the animal in a ritual way to send the spirit of the animal back

Buffalo dance of the Mandans. Artwork by Karl Bodmer, 1833-34.

to the Chief Animal Spirit. The Chief Animal Spirit will then recreate animal life and the hunter will be fed once again.

Hunting Rituals

Today, some Cherokee peoples of North Carolina recite prayer songs the evening before a hunt. They go to the river to pray to the two main guardians of hunters—the river, also known as Long Man, and the fire, known as Ancient Red. The hunter also seeks favor from the wind, praying that he find game at a single bend of the river so he won't have to hunt far. Rubbing ashes on his chest before sleeping, the hunter asks for dreams of a successful hunt.

Deer continues to provide food for the Eastern Cherokee, and hunters pray to Little Deer for a good hunt. It is also very important to the Cherokee hunter to pray again after killing a deer, apologizing for having killed one of Little Deer's creatures. He promises to use all of its parts carefully and bury the remains properly. There is a Cherokee belief that if a hunter does not do this, Little Deer will strike him with arthritis and other diseases in revenge for the disrespectful killing of the animal.

Ritual in Other Daily Activities

Farming. For the Hopi of Arizona, planting and harvesting corn are considered sacred experiences. The ceremonies and rituals surrounding corn farming emphasize its sacredness.

In Hopi traditions, the people emerged from the womb of Mother Earth. Just before they emerged they were given a choice of foods. The Hopi chose an ear of corn and became farmers. Since they chose the short blue ear of corn, which is harder to grow, the Hopi chose a life of hardship and humility. At the same time, blue corn is the most durable kind of corn, meaning that the Hopi chose a hearty life as well. The symbolism of blue corn runs throughout Hopi religious life. According to Emory Sekaquaptewa, a Hopi elder, blue corn is the Hopi law. In growing blue corn, the Hopi are following the law laid down in the Beginning of Time, when they first chose a hard but meaningful life.

Making Fire. When a Kaska Indian makes fire by striking two stones together, he performs a religious ritual. For although the rock seems to be a lifeless and inactive object, it can create a phenomenon that no human being can accomplish on his or her own. The rock resists human will at first, but eventually gives the gift of fire. Production of fire, an act of creation, is likened to the creation of the universe by the Kaska.

The Sacredness of Native American Buildings

Throughout Native North America, buildings and houses carry religious meaning. Although most Native Americans no longer live in traditional houses, some do. Some traditional houses are now maintained for cultural and ceremonial purposes.

Among the Pawnee, the traditional earth lodge is built to represent the universe. It is supported by four posts that represent the East, West, North, and South Stars. The ceiling has a ring representing the Corona Bore-alis (a northern group of stars), the circular floor represents earth, and the domed roof symbolizes sky, or Tirawa, "he who lives up there." The earthen altar on the west wall represents the Garden of the Evening Star. In this altar, corncobs symbolize farming and buffalo skulls symbolize hunting. Pawnee children are taught that the lodge is the universe.

Among the Navajo, the six-sided hogan represents the entire universe—east, west, north, south, above, and below. Similar symbolism is found in the houses and underground ceremonial rooms of the Pueblo, and in the teepee and the sweat lodge of the Plains Indians.

Art as Sacred Expression

Native peoples have traditionally held a very different view of art than the European cultures. They do not create art to be studied for its own beauty, or to be a lasting testament to the skills or vision of the artist. Native American artists frequently attempt to express the rhythms of life that they experience. For them, human beings are not the center of attention. Traditional American Indian art does not emphasize the drama of human existence so much as it illuminates humans' role in life.

Although Indian art has recently become very popular among non-Indians, much of what Westerners consider Indian art is actually created for other reasons. Among the Hopi, kachina dolls created for children are discarded in dumps when no longer useful. The Navajo are known for their beautiful sand paintings, but these are created as part of important healing rituals. At the end of the ceremony, the sand paintings are often destroyed because they have served their purpose and are no longer needed. Much American Indian art is done in wood because wood does not last. It cracks, splinters, and turns back into what it once was, like other cycles of life.

American Indian artists often try to uncover a form that is already present in the material they use rather than imposing their wills onto an object. For example, a Seri Indian from Baja, California, takes a block of ironwood in order to carve a roadrunner. He sees the roadrunner's form in the wood and then chips away the extra wood to reveal the form that is already present. In this way, the artist engages in a religious activity because he feels that a sacred power revealed the form to him.

Music is also revealed to the people by sacred powers. Both Hopi and Sioux musicians have said that they compose music by listening to the sounds of nature. By listening to wind and water, they find musical patterns that already exist, and then use their musical instruments to reproduce those sounds. Instead of creating music, they discover it.

American Indian Clowns

Among the Teton Lakota (a Sioux tribe in South Dakota), there is a secret society of men who have dreamed of the Thunderbird, a powerful spirit. These men, called *Heyoka* (or "Fool"), participate in special ceremonies where they do everything backwards. The clown walks backwards, weeps for joy, wears heavy clothing in the summer, washes with sand, and dries with water. By acting contrary to normal behavior, the Heyoka reveals the nature of ordinary life

Charlie Ugyuk, an Inuit carver, carving soapstone, Northwest Territory.

by contrast. This is but a small part of the total ceremony, which involves sacred ritual and prayer. Today only a few traditional Sioux perform this ritual.

Among the Hopi and other Pueblo Indians, clowns perform various skits to show such vices as gluttony (the habit of overeating), selfishness, and ignorance. The crowd watching these ceremonies laughs at the foolishness of the clowns. At the same time, the observers are also laughing at themselves, because the clowns are demonstrating what people are really like—not what they should be like. Among the Pueblo, clowning ceremonies are still performed frequently in the summer months. They are

Hopi Anak'china Dance, clown antics, Oraibi, Arizona, 1912.

conducted along with ceremonies of kachina dancers, who impersonate more solemn aspects of the spiritual world.

Religious Beliefs since European Occupation

In response to European aggression and conquest, Native American peoples have formed new religions. Defeated, hungry, tired, confined to reservations, Native peoples looked for hope in new religions. On the reservations, missionaries of Christian churches often played a large role in the education and social conditions of the Native peoples, as they sought to convert them. Some Native Americans adopted Christianity, but only about 15 percent today consider themselves fully Christian. Others practice religions that blend the old and new ways—combining Christianity or other religions with traditional Native beliefs and practices.

Christian Missionaries

From Christopher Columbus's first expedition to the New World in 1492, Europeans planned to convert Native North Americans to Christianity. Roman Catholic missionaries took an active role in the earliest settlements and explorations of the Americas. French Catholic priests of the Jesuit order arrived in New France in the early 1600s to try to convert Indian nations such as the

The restored church at San Ildefonso Pueblo.

Naskapi, the Montagnais, the Malicite, the Huron, and the Iroquois. They attempted to found a mission near Montreal in which Indians would live in a monastery-like style. The mission failed for a number of reasons, but the Jesuit priests remained until 1760, living among the Indian nations and seeking converts.

Many of the Jesuits learned to appreciate the differences among cultures. Some were willing to tolerate the continuing practice of traditional religions among their converts. France's Jesuit priests made many lasting converts to Christianity. Their letters provide some of the earliest historical material on the Indian nations of North America.

The Spanish justified their conquest of Indians as a means to convert them to Christianity and save their souls. The Spanish established their earliest missions in Florida. In the early 1600s, the Spanish moved into the Southwest, building missions among the Pueblo communities along the Rio Grande. They proceeded to exploit Indian workers while they attempted to convert them to Christianity. The Pueblo Indians revolted against Spanish rule in 1680, temporarily driving the Spanish out of the area, because they did not want to accept Catholicism and Hispanic culture as their own. Spanish rule was restored in 1696, and the Pueblo were forced to accept the strong presence of the Catholic church. Many Pueblo communities and individuals became outwardly Christian.

By the early 1700s they were practicing Catholicism in public, but all the while, traditional religious practices were conducted secretly. Even today, many Pueblo choose to protect their religious rituals and ceremonies from outsiders' view.

The Spanish missionaries in California sought to take the Natives off their traditional lands and move them into mission stations where they would live Christian lives in service to the church. From 1769 to the 1820s, the Spanish missions worked to destroy Native cultures, to discourage Native ceremonies and traditions, to discourage the use of Native languages, and to force Indians to adopt Christianity. Many Natives died because of the difficult work and poor health conditions, and the harsh policies led to the destruction of many tribal traditions and communities.

The British Puritans actively taught Christianity to the Indians in New England. By 1676, however, war and disease had wiped out much of the Native population. The few who remained in New England were given the choice of migrating to unknown territories or accepting colonial rule, a European lifestyle, and Christianity. The settlements of the Indians who stayed were often called "praying towns."

In the early 1800s, a Protestant revival known as the Second Great Awakening spread across the United States. Presbyterians, Baptists, Quakers, Methodists, and many other Christian denominations actively sought conversions among the Indian peoples. The missionaries secured funding from the U.S. government and carried out the government's plans to "civilize" the Indians by converting them to Christianity and teaching them the lifestyle, culture, and economics of American society.

In the twentieth century, many Indian communities in Canada and the United States are, to varying extents, Christian. But for many Christian Native peoples, Christianity has not in any way replaced Indian spirituality. Among the northern Cheyenne, who live on a reservation in eastern Montana, the elders of the tribe say that it is possible for a person to practice the Sun Dance, a traditional renewal ceremony, and also follow the Christian faith and attend the ceremonies of the Native American Church. In the Northern Cheyenne view, there is more than one way to communicate with the spiritual side of life; one is allowed to pursue more than one path. The ceremonies, however, are not mixed but kept separate and pure in their own spheres.

Other communities, such as the Iroquois of upstate New York, do not wish to accept Western European religion into their community. In the early 1800s, Christian missionaries demanded complete social, cultural, and religious conversion—a total rejection of Iroquois culture. Many Iroquois saw, and still see, Christianity as a threat to the survival of the Iroquois culture.

Native American Church

Peyote is obtained from button-like parts of a small cactus grown in Texas and northern Mexico. People eat it to stimulate their perceptions and to enhance concentration and the experience of religious truths during ceremonies. Although peyote is not addictive, it is treated as a controlled substance in most states.

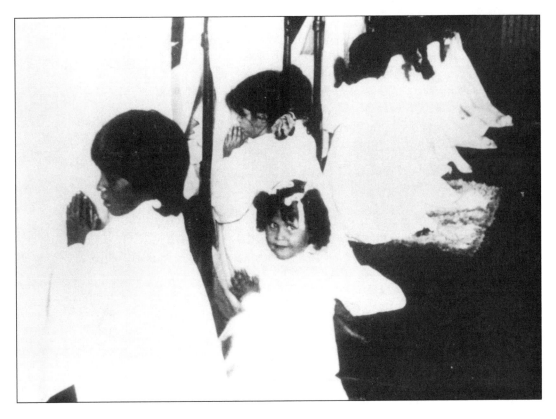

Little girls praying beside their beds, Phoenix Indian School, Arizona, 1900.

The peyote religion has a long history among Native North American peoples. It became widespread in the 1880s, when many Indian peoples had been defeated by the U.S. Army and confined to reservations. The U.S. government had basically outlawed Native religions. The peyote religion offered Indian people a way to regain their cultural identity and restore themselves. The peyote religion also blended Christianity with traditional beliefs, so that followers no longer needed to choose between the two conflicting religions.

John Wilson, a man of mixed Delaware, Caddo, and French parentage who is credited with spreading the new religion, adopted the peyote religion in 1880. Wilson claimed to have had several revelations instructing him on ceremonial procedures. He reported being transported to the "sky realm," where he learned of events in Jesus Christ's life and of the spirit forces, such as the sun, moon, and fire. Wilson said that the Peyote Road, which led from Christ's grave to the moon, is the road Christ traveled in his ascent into Heaven. To follow the Peyote Road means to follow the way of Christ's teaching. One learned about Christ and purged oneself of sins through use of peyote.

In the Native American Church people

could confess their sins and ask forgiveness. Members were encouraged to give up alcohol and follow Christian principles of brotherhood. At the same time, Native Americans could communicate with the Creator through visions, as in Native American religions. Curing ceremonies, the vision quest, and other traditional rituals were also used.

In 1918, several peyote groups formed the Native American Church in Oklahoma. In 1954, with the formation of the Native American Church of Canada, the Native American Church became international. By the 1970s, there were as many as 250,000 Indian members. The Native American Church is the largest and fastest-growing Indian religion in North America.

The Native American Church remains controversial because of its use of peyote. Peyote is an illegal substance except for its use in Indian religious ceremonies, and even then permits must be given by the U.S. attorney general's office. In fact, the use of peyote is a misdemeanor in 24 states. Offenders can receive sentences of up to one year in jail and fines from $2,000 to $5,000. In 1990, a U.S. Supreme Court decision left it up to the various states to decide whether peyote could be used as a religious sacrament. Many Native Americans today feel that their religious freedoms continue to be denied because of this ruling.

Revitalization Movements

Several prophets, or religious leaders, emerged among Native Americans during the 1800s to offer hope to their downtrodden people. Because the prophets' teachings offered ways for Indian people to renew themselves, they became known as

NATIVE AMERICAN PROPHETS

Prophets and prophecy are an important part of Native American religions. A prophet traditionally arises to give the people hope and direction in times of crisis. Many Native American prophets had visions during a severe illness in which they "died" for a time and then came back to life, bearing a message from the spirit world they had just visited. Most prophecies of the eighteenth and nineteenth centuries directed Indian peoples to go back to the old way of life that existed before the Europeans settled in North America. Prophecies also provided new religious practices and beliefs needed to fight against the evils of non-Indian society, such as alcohol, lying, and cheating. The prophecies often promised that the spiritual world would help the Indian peoples by restoring the old order and ridding the continent of colonial rule. Some prophecies recommended military resistance to U.S. authority, while others advised nonviolence.

"revitalization" movements. The Handsome Lake Movement and the Ghost Dance Movement are well-known examples. Other movements were led by prophets such as Tenskwatawa (Shawnee), Sweet Medicine (Cheyenne), and Smohalla (Wanapum).

The Handsome Lake Movement

By the late 1700s, the Iroquois had been dispersed to reservations, where conditions led to rising alcoholism and alarming rates of depression and suicide. Iroquois villages had become slums in the wilderness. In looking for a solution the Iroquois saw two paths, either to adopt the American culture or to resist and preserve the traditional ways. In 1799, a former Iroquois warrior and chief, Handsome Lake, arose as a prophet. He had a vision and, speaking an ancient form of Iroquois, called his people to renew themselves.

Handsome Lake condemned drinking, violence, and sexual promiscuity as enemies of Native American family life. He stressed traditional values and the need for collective well-being. He taught the Iroquois to tolerate American culture, but with caution. Handsome Lake stressed the Christian ideas of God, sin, repentance, and salvation. At the same time, he also encouraged the traditional rituals, especially those that gave thanks to the powers of the universe upon whom people depended. One result of Handsome Lake's work was the establishment in the 1830s of the longhouse religion, a uniquely Iroquois faith and practice.

The Ghost Dance Movement and Wounded Knee

The Ghost Dance movement originated in the 1870s among the Northern Paiute when Wodziwob ("White Hair") had a vision that a big train would bring back the dead Indian ancestors. In this vision, the United States would be wiped out, but Indians and the land would remain. Then, the Great Spirit would return. New songs and religious dancing were performed to hasten this event. After a time this early Ghost Dance movement faded.

In 1889 a new prophet, Wovoka, arose among the Paiute. Wovoka was born at Pyramid Lake, Nevada, the son of a Paiute leader and "weather doctor"—one who can control the weather. Wovoka, too, became a weather doctor and led the traditional circle dances. Between dances he preached universal love. Wovoka worked for a time with a non-Indian rancher and became familiar with the Christian Bible.

On January 1, 1889, a total eclipse of the sun occurred, and Wovoka, while very ill, experienced a powerful vision. When the sun "died" that day, he reported being taken up to Heaven, where God gave him a message of peace and right living. As word of this vision spread, Wovoka became known as a powerful prophet. Even the Mormon settlers in the area thought for a while that Wovoka might be the messiah prophesied by their founder. Wovoka taught a new circle dance to "embrace Our Father, God."

Wovoka explained that non-Indians had been sent to punish Indians for their sins, but that the punishment would soon end. He foresaw that a tremendous disaster would befall the U.S. settlers, who would disappear from the continent. Long-dead Indian ancestors and game would then return, and the old Indian world would be restored. Until the old world returned, however, it could be visited through a new religious dance, by wearing religious costumes, singing Ghost songs, and entering into self-hypnotic trances.

199

Arapaho Ghost Dance.

During a Ghost Dance, a dancer would fall down in a trance, "dying." Afterwards, he or she would speak of traveling to the moon or the morning star. Sometimes the dancer came back holding strange rocks that were said to be "star flesh." Through these trances, one could "visit" the long-dead relatives and see the promised world. Followers of the Ghost Dance movement anxiously awaited the disaster that would mark the end of U.S. inhabitation of North America. This was supposed to happen sometime in 1890.

Wovoka's message spread quickly among the Lakota Sioux. The Great Sioux Nation had been broken up, and the sacred Black Hills had been seized for their gold deposits. By 1889 the Sioux were dying of starvation due to a severe drought. Food rations promised by Congress were slow in coming, and disease epidemics ravaged the popula-

Arapaho Ghost Dance. Artwork by Mary Irvin Wright, c. 1900, based on photographs by James Mooney.

tion. Sioux holy men took up the Ghost Dance as a form of spiritual resistance to U.S. authority. It was said that warriors wearing ghost shirts could turn back soldier's bullets.

The U.S. government's Indian police and agents, fearing that the Ghost Dance movement would lead to a major Indian uprising, set out to vigorously suppress the new religion. Sitting Bull, one of the principal Sioux leaders who sympathized with the Ghost Dance movement, was assassinated by Indian police. After Sitting Bull's assassination, terrified Ghost Dance followers fled to the Pine Ridge Reservation in South Dakota to seek protection. On December 24, 1890, just miles from Pine Ridge at Wounded Knee Creek, the Seventh Cavalry of the U.S. Army opened fire on the Indians with machine guns. These guns shot rounds at the rate of nearly fifty a minute, mowing down everything alive—warriors, old people, women, children, ponies, and dogs. Of the 370 Indians massacred that day, 250 were women and children.

Revitalization Movements Today

During the 1960s and 1970s Native Americans in the cities of North America began a political movement resisting U.S. authority and paternalism (treating Indians as wards or children) and seeking self-gov-

Revival of the Ghost Dance, May 1974.

ernment and land and fishing rights. In the 1980s and 1990s there was a new movement of religious and cultural revitalization on the reservations. Native American religions have become a center of what it means to be Indian for many Native Americans.

Sweat lodges have been set up in the prisons. The use of sacred pipes and the purification ceremonies of the Sun Dance are spreading throughout the United States. The Native American Church has become an increasingly important form of therapy and recovery for that part of the Indian population suffering from alcohol and drug addiction. Not only traditional religion, but also native Indian languages, singing and drumming, long suppressed ritual practices (like "piercing" as a form of sacrifice in the Sun Dance), storytelling and the oral traditions, have all seen a revival.

16
Native Economics

Native Economic Systems Before Columbus

No written records document the economic systems of Native North America before the Europeans came. Pre-Columbian North American history spans many eras and geographic areas and includes a great variety of cultural groups. One thing we can be certain about is that there were many different ways that Native American peoples worked and organized their labors.

In the large and complex societies of the Southwest and Mississippi River valley, there were probably many kinds of work and very specific ways of **dividing labor** among members of the community. Certain types of work may have been assigned by gender (depending on whether the person was male or female) or by membership in a family or clan. The large societies of the South and Southwest were probably hierarchical, meaning that members were ranked by their status in the group. The most unpleasant and disagreeable tasks were given to those in the lowest social ranks. Some of these societies even took slaves from enemy villages and gave them the most undesirable jobs. The larger societies were able to produce enough "extra" goods to allow some members to practice art, medicine, or religion on a full-time basis.

Small hunting and gathering societies also inhabited much of North America. Many were **nomadic** (traveling and relocating often, usually in search of food and other resources or a better climate). These societies had more simple ways of assigning work to members. Although gender and social position were still important in assigning tasks, many hunting and gathering groups spent most of their time working to provide food, shelter, and clothing for survival. Small societies usually could not produce extra goods (an economic surplus) to support members to work in medicine or art on a full-time basis. They also could not trade with other communities located far away.

Whether simple or complex, most Native American economies were based on a concept of community well-being rather than individual prosperity. Many groups of Native American were adept traders before and after the Europeans came to North America who were skilled at bargaining and obtaining desired goods. But in most Native American cultures, this work was aimed at promoting the well-being of the entire village or community. Personal wealth was not a measure of success. In fact, for many groups personal wealth was considered a sign of greed. Personal status was increased by giving away material goods rather than by owning them. Even today "giveaway" ceremonies, called potlatches by some groups, are a central feature of Native cultures. In these ceremonies, a person or family giving presents to others increases their standing in the community.

In American Indian trade before Europeans arrived, goods may have been traded in simple exchanges—a piece of pottery traded for a piece of leather, for example. Forms of money, such as **wampum,** were also used. Wampum was made by stringing together particular types of sea shells. Like money, wampum was obtained by selling something and could be used later to buy something else. Some groups engaged in long-distance trading. Goods have been found far from the places where they were produced. For example, there was trade between Cahokia (a large city near present-day St. Louis) and many cities in what is now Mexico.

An Era of Profitable Trade with Europeans

When Europeans and Native Americans first met in about 1500, they were fairly equal trading partners with different abilities and products. Europeans could travel long distances over the ocean; Indians could travel easily over long stretches of land. Indians had advanced crops, such as corn, cotton, and potatoes. They also had gold and

How They Till the Soil and Plant. Drawing by Le Moyne, engraving from Theodore de Bry, *America,* Part II, 1591.

silver. Europeans could offer useful animal power in horses, oxen, and cattle. They also produced guns, knives, and other weapons and metal tools.

Productive trade started immediately. The flow of gold and silver to Europe supported the growth there of large trading companies. Horses, guns, and metal goods dramatically changed the way Native North Americans lived. Manufactured goods made Indian hunters more efficient. They could kill more game and do it more easily. Metal pots, needles, and other domestic goods also changed women's work. Income levels of both American Indians and Europeans rose because of the trade between them.

New trade networks with the English, French, and Spanish created enormous demand for Native American goods. Furs and other animal skins, for example, were highly valued in Europe. Indian hunters used weapons and traps made in Europe to kill animals for the furs they traded to the fur companies. The period from 1600 until about 1750 is known as the mercantile period—a time when Indians and Europeans maintained a more or less equal position in their profitable trade relationships, based primarily on hunting resources.

During the entire mercantile era, two different ways of managing land and resources coexisted. Most Indians thought of a hunting area as the property of a whole community. Usually someone within the community who understood those resources advised everyone on their use. Europeans, on the other hand, saw resources such as hunting areas in one of two ways: either as private property owned by an individual, or as open access where anyone could hunt without regard to traditional territorial control. During the mercantile era, many Native American groups managed to maintain their community- or family-controlled resources and trade successfully with Europeans, who sought private profit. The two very different economic systems usually did not conflict with each other.

For example, in the southeastern part of what is now the United States, Indian tribes such as the Cherokee, Choctaw, Chickasaw, and Creek lived in towns. The chiefs of these towns collected corn, squash, and other products from the members of the town. The chiefs then used the products they had collected to care for people who needed food and to trade for needed goods from Europe. They alternated trading with the French and the British, depending on which offered the best trade value. The chiefs served as the go-betweens in the trade deals. They obtained the European goods and distributed them to the members of their towns. Their societies were based on giving and receiving gifts, and leaders gave the most.

Indian enterprise, unlike European or later U.S. enterprise, was based on the family, clan, or town structure of each Indian nation. When families controlled territory, business was conducted by the family. When a town controlled a territory, business was conducted by the leadership of the town.

Near James Bay in Canada, the Cree managed their community resources by family-controlled areas. Each family hunting area had a "boss" responsible for selling or distributing the furs obtained in hunting the area. Non-family members could hunt for food in these areas, but the hides of the animals killed belonged to the family, who traded them for European manufactured goods.

In the Pacific Northwest, community resource management was significant in organizing the salmon harvest. Northwestern elders decided who could take salmon and how much they could take at the customary fishing camps located on the major rivers. The elders of the Tlingit in southern Alaska managed the fishing, hunting, and trading in their area.

During the mercantile era, the European and the Native American cultures came to understand each other's way of trading. Europeans gave gifts in return for beaver. Indians understood the effects of prices. If the French were giving fewer gifts for beaver skins, Indians would take their beaver pelts to the English.

The distinctive feature of the mercantile era is that Indian governments retained considerable power over large areas of North America. Europeans managed their use of the land through the system of private property and personal gain. Their control was confined mainly to the coastal areas. Indian methods of using land through community control were strong in other areas, where trade involved the exchange of gifts. And in other regions where there was a mixture of Indian and European control, compromise allowed both types of land use to coexist.

Storing Their Crops in the Public Granary. Drawing by John White and Jacques Le Moyne and engraved by T. de Bry.

The Balance of Power Shifts

Changes on both sides of the Atlantic Ocean ended the mercantile period. In Europe the agricultural revolution resulted in a rapid increase in the Europeans' ability to grow food. This was largely a result of the introduction of potatoes to cold areas of Europe. The industrial revolution began in England in the mid-1700s. By 1750, England had discovered the usefulness of organizing work in factories. They were able to produce enough food to allow labor to leave the farms, they had a trade network with North America that provided raw materials, and they had learned how to use coal as fuel to run their factories.

The industrial revolution also had a dramatic impact on North America. Small, individually owned farms were replaced by large-scale agriculture, which was needed for the new industrial society. Just as workers were needed for the factories, land was needed for commercial use. By the early 1800s, American cotton was sold to English mills to be made into cloth. This meant that additional land was needed for cotton in the South. In the North, timber was needed for building cities. As large cities developed, commercial agriculture—as opposed to individual farmers—was needed to produce large amounts of food and other resources for the growing populations.

Most Native American **economies** remained based on agriculture and the products of wild lands, forest, and prairies, while the European economies became industrially based. Indian economies had become increasingly based on trade of fur and food with Europeans. As they were forced from their lands and had to compete with non-Indian hunters on lands that remained available, Native Americans were frequently pushed out of trade. Even as late as 1800, Indians were holding their own with the European merchants. However, the industrial revolution, along with diseases introduced by Europeans, began a period of devastating losses for the Indians during the 1800s.

Between 1500 and 1800, the number of Native Americans fell from over five million to less than one million. [Also see U.S. Native American Populations and Their Lands chapter.] In contrast, the colonist population had increased to five million. More and more land was needed for agriculture and for the increasing colonial population. At the same time, the new United States republic had adopted a policy of "Manifest Destiny." This meant populating America from coast to coast with settlers (Europeans). In the 1800s, many European immigrants came to the United States and migrated west in search of farm land.

In Georgia, the Cherokee managed to stay in their homelands for many years after the industrial revolution. They developed plantations and sold cotton, building a strong economy on their lands. Envious non-Indian neighbors began to do everything they could, including using military force, to remove the Cherokee and take over their lands. This kind of thing was happening throughout the South. The policy of removing Indians was formally adopted by the United States government in 1830. As a result, Indians were removed by force from the entire eastern United States to areas west of the Mississippi River. Most were resettled in present-day Oklahoma and Kansas.

By the mid-1800s, most Indians had been moved from the East to reservations west of the Mississippi, although those who lived in the West and Pacific Northwest continued the lifestyles and patterns of trade that had existed during the mercantile period.

Originally, the reservations were intended to be used only by Indians. In 1887, however, the Dawes General Allotment Act was passed by Congress. This act imposed private ownership of land on the Indians. Instead of community land management, land was divided up and small parcels were given to each family. Many families who had once farmed together found that their parcels were not located next to each other. The parcels were too small to be very productive, and Indians did not have the money to buy the cattle or farm equipment they needed.

In addition, some reservation lands—usually the best and most productive—were given to non-Indians. Large-scale commercial agriculture (farming to produce large amounts of food for sale) was primarily non-Indian. The American economy that was developing excluded Indian enterprise more and more. As a result of the government's success in removing Indians from mainstream American life, Indians developed very few skills with which to join the new work force. They were often forced to settle for unskilled labor such as farm work, clearing brush, or digging ditches.

As more non-Indians entered Indian lands, the non-Indian **open access** system of land control overran Indian methods of communal management of their property. Until this time, Indians had been able to protect their animal resources by limiting harvests when they hunted. This prevented extinction. Under open access, however, anyone could hunt animals. By 1890, the huge herds of buffalo were wiped out, and the American bison narrowly escaped extinction. Because of the destruction of the buffalo, Plains people were left without a means of support.

In the Pacific Northwest, Indians who lived by catching salmon found that very few salmon were reaching their traditional fishing sites. Non-Indians, who used boats to harvest salmon upstream, caught the fish first.

In the late 1800s the United States also embarked on a policy of forcing Indians to give up their tribal cultures. From 1890 to 1934, the government tried to "civilize" the Indians. One of the ways they tried to accomplish this was by forcing Indians to adopt non-Indian farming practices. Some Indians successfully took up farming or ranching. But many Indian men, used to a lifestyle of hunting and fishing, rejected farming. Non-Indians who moved onto the reservations had several important advantages. They had money to buy equipment and to develop their businesses, and the court system was usually on their side when disputes arose. Non-Indians usually controlled the stores on reservations.

WORDS TO KNOW

capitalism: a type of economy in which property and businesses are owned by individuals or groups of individuals (rather than being owned by the government or by the society as a whole). Profits in a *capitalist* economy are based on competition and enrich the individual owner. Workers are paid a wage, or an agreed-upon amount, for their efforts.

cooperative: a type of business in which members share in the profits and losses; sometimes called a co-op. As the name implies, *cooperatives* are based on the cooperation of members; they aim to increase the wealth of the whole group, not just certain individuals.

division of labor: dividing up, or sharing, different kinds of work among the people of a society.

economic development: the process of creating or improving a society's economy. Starting small businesses like stores or restaurants, building a factory, or establishing job training programs are examples of *economic development* in modern American culture. The goal of *economic development* is to increase the wealth of the community and to improve the people's standard of living.

Originally, reservations were a fairly good environment for Indians to practice traditional community-based business methods within an industrial country where private property and personal gain ruled. Many

Apaches delivering hay at Fort Apache.

groups began business enterprises on the reservations when they were removed to them. But a century of extremely harsh and constantly shifting government policies, including allotment, assimilation, termination, and broken treaties, caused many reservation enterprises to fail.

A few tribal enterprises have managed to survive. The Menominee lumber mill in Wisconsin is one example. The Menominee owned forested lands. Because they received external political support, the U.S. government did not force them to divide up their lands. But the experience of the Menominee is a special case. For the most part, the industrial revolution caused mas-

sive declines in Indian land ownership and economic activity.

Reservation Economics

To say that poverty has existed on Indian reservations throughout their history does not fully describe the situation. By the 1890s, the U.S. government's Bureau of Indian Affairs (BIA) had undermined the ability of Indians to support and govern themselves. The BIA assigned agents to run the reservations. These Indian agents often controlled the reservations with the help of the more "Americanized" tribal leaders. Power was transferred to these leaders, who were often manipulated by the BIA to serve U.S. policy rather than the interests of the tribe. In some cases, the Indian leaders were corrupt and used their positions to serve their own needs, rather than those of the community. As a result, Native Americans were frequently unable to trust the leadership of their reservations.

A large and important study of American Indian conditions, called the Meriam Report, was conducted in 1928. The report stated that poverty among Indians in the United States was related to three main causes:

1) The destruction of the Indians' traditional culture and economy,

2) The fundamental differences between Native American social systems and the U.S. economic system,

3) Past policies of the U.S. government.

Although the government set out to provide the food, clothing, education, and medicine they had promised to the conquered Indian nations, the government's management of Indian affairs often had the ulterior purpose of acquiring Indian land and natural resources for settlers. Impoverishment and inadequate means of supporting themselves caused Indians to become dependent on the government. Because of this economic dependence, the BIA grew into a powerful force on reservations.

Between 1929 and 1941 the Great Depression (a period when the U.S. economy did poorly and many people found themselves out of work) forced many Indian farmers and ranchers out of business. President Franklin D. Roosevelt designed programs such as the

---

WORDS TO KNOW

economy: a society's system for producing, distributing, and using goods.

nomadic: traveling and relocating often, usually in search of food and other resources or a better climate.

open access: a European concept of land use in the sixteenth and seventeenth centuries in which it was held that any area that was not legally owned by an individual or other legal party could be used for hunting or obtaining other resources without regard to traditional territorial control.

travois: a hauling vehicle made of two long poles that bear a platform or net to carry loads. Before the Spanish brought horses to North America, many Native groups used dogs to pull the *travois.*

wampum: small blue and white beads made from shells. Long strings of *wampum* were used as trade exchange among some Native American groups.

Works Project Administration (WPA) to help people who couldn't find work. Roosevelt's "New Deal" programs helped many Indians, as well as non-Indians, through this difficult period. As a part of the New Deal administration, the Indian Reorganization Act (IRA), passed in 1934, put a stop to land allotment practices. The IRA allowed Indians to create constitutions and governments, as well as develop their own economic systems. Only about 92 reservations adopted IRA tribal government constitutions under the plan, and

Office and sutler store. Round Valley Agency, California, 1897.

about 45 formed **economic development** corporations. Despite the intentions of the IRA, tribal governments did not gain significant power over the way money was spent within the reservation or over the leasing of their lands. The BIA closely controlled these developments and frequently overruled tribal council decisions. During the 1930s little real political freedom or economic growth occurred.

During World War II, many Indians joined the armed forces, and others moved to urban areas to work in defense plants. After the war, many remained in the cities to seek opportunities not available on the reservations. In the early 1990s only 22 per-

cent of the Native American population of the United States lived on reservations.

During the 1950s, the government planned to abolish reservations and integrate Indians into mainstream American society, encouraging the urbanization process that was already taking place. Both Indians and state governments resisted, and the policy was ended by 1960. During the 1960s and 1970s, efforts were made to provide loans and promote the economies of reservations. This funding expanded tribal governments and increased opportunities for training and education. However, this led to only a few major economic projects that were owned and operated by Indians. From 1980 to 1992,

Cartoon criticizing mismanagement of Indian affairs by politically appointed Indian agents.

government funding was severely cut back, and tribal governments were once again left with few resources.

After so many years of being vulnerable to the tremendous shifts in public policy toward Native Americans, many Indian leaders today focus on strengthening tribal governments and independent economic bases on the Indian reservations. Reservations face a major challenge in using their resources to create jobs, provide higher standards of living, and improve social conditions for their members. The changes tak-ing place offer some hope of breaking the cycles of poverty that plague so many Indian communities.

The Indian Self-Determination and Education Assistance Act was passed in 1975. This act gives tribal governments the power to arrange for services once provided by the BIA. Reservations are seeking development in a number of different business efforts: energy and mining, agriculture and livestock, forestry, gambling and entertainment, tourism and hotels, arts and crafts, and manufacturing and assembly.

Indian airmen performing a mock Indian dance for their fellow servicemen during World War II.

Energy and Mining

Over 200 billion tons of coal, or 13 percent of the total U.S. reserves, are found on Indian reservations in the West. Reservation lands also account for about 4.2 billion barrels of oil and 17.5 trillion cubic feet of natural gas. Uranium is an important mineral resource on some reservations, particularly for the Navajo and Laguna Pueblo tribes.

These energy resources provide significant income for the 42 members of the Council of Energy Resource Tribes (CERT). CERT is an organization of Indian tribes formed to negotiate and oversee the sale and use of oil, gas, coal, and minerals. CERT was formed in response to previous BIA policies that sold Indian resources well below market value. For example, on the Navajo and Hopi reservations, coal companies were given 50-year leases at less that 50 cents per ton at a time when the market price was over $70 per ton! There have been frequent incidents in which royalties that should have been paid to the tribes were stolen or not reported. The Wind River Reservation in Wyoming, for example, lost over $750,000 in oil royalties during a nine-year period.

Although tribes receive royalties from the sale of their resources, minerals have not always brought the prosperity they could to the tribe. Many of the jobs in the oil and coal-mining industries require skills that people on reservations usually don't have. Also, many of the higher-paying jobs are given to union members rather than local workers.

Resource Management

There are more than 54 million acres of Indian land. About 42 million acres of this land are owned by tribes, and about 11 million acres are owned, under BIA control, by individuals. Most of these lands have been so fragmented by past government policies, they do not represent the same opportunities that they might otherwise. In addition, Native American lands cannot be used as collateral to back up a loan. This makes it very difficult for Indian landowners to get loans for farm equipment, seeds, and fertilizer.

In 1983 Congress passed the Indian Land Consolidation Act to help reduce the fragmentation of Indian lands. Over time, this may help improve the usability of the lands. Tribes like the Mille Lacs Band of Chippewa in Minnesota have started a Land Pur-

A logging truck hauls ponderosa pine into the logging yard for lumber process at Navajo Forest Products Industry at Navajo, New Mexico.

chase Trust Fund to help restore their 61,000 acre reservation.

Some reservations lease land to non-Indian farmers and ranchers, or issue mineral leases to large non-Indian companies. The leasing of Indian land created income of about $68 million in 1984. Oil, gas, coal, and other mineral leases provided over $230 million.

Today tribal leaders on reservations realize the importance of developing their economies in a way that will preserve their traditional cultures. For example, five Indian pueblos in New Mexico formed an organization to grow and sell blue corn, a traditional food. Cattle and sheep ranching, fishing, and truck farming create jobs that are in accord with Indian traditions. However, these jobs are often low-paying and seasonal.

Forestry

Of the 54 million acres of land owned by American Indians, about 5.3 million acres have valuable timber. This is roughly 1.5 percent of the country's total supply. Although 57 reservations earn money through forestry, only about 14 have enough timber for commercial operations. In most cases, tribes harvest the timber and send it to mills outside the reservations for processing. Timber harvesting is supervised by the BIA, and much mismanagement of funds has been reported. The BIA misplaced as much as $500,000 per year of income for the Red Lake Chippewa of Minnesota. In other cases, BIA accounts have not been balanced in over 70 years.

Gambling and Entertainment

In 1979 there were no significant bingo or gambling casinos on Indian reservations. By the early 1990s, gambling income for Indian reservations was about $5.5 billion. Indian gambling accounts for a small portion of the total U.S. gambling revenues, which total about $350 billion. Nevertheless, gambling has become a leading source of income for Indians.

At least half of the Indian tribes in the U.S. have bingo operations, and Indians run at least 40 casinos in about 12 states. The Federal Indian Gambling Regulatory Act of 1988 allows any tribe recognized by the U.S. government to engage in gambling activities. Reservation governments use income from gambling to support their elderly and sick members and to pay for health care, housing, and other improvements. Some tribes have bought back ancient lands, restored sacred areas, worked to preserve traditional culture, established scholarship funds, and created jobs with income from the gambling industry. Although not all tribes agree that gambling is a good type of development, to many tribes without other resources it is a necessary means to generate income.

Tourism and Hotels

During the late 1960s, the Economic Development Administration provided money for tribes to build hotels and restaurants. Many of these did not generate the income that was expected. Some of these facilities were built too far from major highways to draw enough visitors. Others went bankrupt because of poor management. An exception is the Kah-Nee-Ta resort on the Warm Springs reservation in Oregon.

Some tribes have been successful in developing tourism, such as the Eastern Cherokee of North Carolina. Their annual play, *Unto These Hills,* portrays Cherokee life during forced removal to the West in the late 1830s. This increases understanding of Indian history and culture for large non-Indian audiences. Powwows and ceremonies are often opened to the public. The Crow Fair held near the Custer Battle Ground in Montana, for example, is a powwow that is well-attended by Indians and non-Indians alike. Income from tourism provides money for tribal museums, art galleries, and annual powwows.

Arts and Crafts

Indian crafts such as jewelry, pottery, and woven textiles have become familiar to most Americans. Usually arts and crafts provide only a small addition to Indian incomes, and rarely become more than small-scale industries.

There is often controversy among Indians over whether Indians should sell objects to non-Indians, especially if the objects have meaning in sacred ceremonies. Most art objects used in ceremonies have traditionally been destroyed after the ceremony was finished. For example, the Hopi create paintings of Kachina spirits for one ceremony only, after which they are destroyed. The Navajo of the Southwest use sandpaintings in curing ceremonies, to help a Native healer restore

Overall view of electronic manufacturing on the electrical harness assembly line inside Chih To Industries Incorporated at Sanders, Arizona.

harmony and balance to a patient. After the curing ceremony, the paintings are destroyed. Many of these are attractive, however, and tourists have often offered to buy them. Needing the money, some Navajo have sold sandpaintings in which they intentionally created small mistakes. In this way they "broke" the painting's sacred power and preserved sacred knowledge, while at the same time were able to sell them as art objects.

Although some Indian art brings high prices, most Indian artists receive only a small fraction of the final selling price. Art dealers and distributors, who make the most profit, are rarely Indians themselves.

Manufacturing and Assembly

The federal government has tried to encourage private companies to build manufacturing facilities on reservations. As a result, thousands of new jobs have been created in the manufacture of clothing, electronics, and other consumer goods. Many reservation jobs, however, are filled by non-Indians. Indians often find the structure of these jobs to be out of touch with their lives on the reservation and their traditional values. Turnover (people leaving jobs) is high as a result. Some tribes have changed their traditions to fit the demands of a forty-hour-a-week job. For example, the Tlingit of Alaska have traditional potlatches (ceremonies) that have traditionally lasted at least four weeks. Today, few working Tlingit can afford to take that much time off work. Most potlatches have been modified to start on Friday evening at dinner and continue until late Sunday afternoon. This allows villagers to return home in time to resume work on Monday morning.

In general, Indian ceremonies and important festivals do not fall on U.S. or Christian holidays. Indian workers are often forced to choose between keeping their jobs and fulfilling their religious obligations. Members of other religious groups, such as Jews or Muslims, have similar problems. Indians, however, face more complications since there are hundreds of different ceremonial calendars, and most of these are unknown outside the local community.

Often the money to create Indian industries comes from land claims suits against the U.S. government. After receiving $81.5 million to settle land claims, the Passamaquoddy and Penobscot Indians in Maine invested in sever-

A young Navajo welder puts his skills and knowledge to the test at a Transwestern Pipeline Co. training session.

al businesses. The Oglala Sioux of South Dakota purchased a meat-packing plant that produces high-quality beef for restaurants. The Blackfeet of Montana founded the Blackfeet Indian Writing Company, which makes pens, pencils, and markers. This company has generated millions of dollars in sales and provided badly needed jobs. (On the Blackfeet reservation, unemployment usually ranges between 55 and 65 percent.) Dozens of other tribes have followed suit and developed manufacturing opportunities.

U.S. Indian Labor

American Indians face many obstacles in finding work. In 1980, for example, about 17 percent of American Indian men were unemployed, while in the same year, only about 6 percent of white men were jobless. These figures show clearly that American Indians experience more unemployment than do whites. However, the actual rates of unemployment of Indians are actually higher than these figures show. Many Indians do not have full-time jobs. In 1979, for example, over half of the Indians who worked did not work full-time. Many Indians are employed in seasonal jobs in construction or tourism, which involve long periods without work. In 1979, only 57 percent of Amer-

Anishinabe man and woman gather wild rice from canoe in Minnesota.

ican Indians who found full-time work reported working for the whole year.

Lack of education is a major problem in finding work. Some experts feel that Indian youth drop out of school because they see no opportunity for work and therefore have no reason to stay in school. This is especial-ly true in rural reservations, where very few jobs are available.

On many large reservations, unemployment is 20 to 30 percent, while unemployment for the rest of the country is around 7 percent. Some of these reservations are severely distressed. The Blackfeet reserva-

Wayland Large works on spreadsheets at BIA office while on co-op work assignment.

tion in Montana, for example, had an unemployment rate of 37 percent in 1980. Unemployment on reservations skyrocketed after 1981, as a result of federal budget cuts.

For American Indians with skills and education, cities offer more opportunities. American Indians living in cities had an unemployment rate of about 12 percent in 1980. Although this was lower than the rate for those living on reservations, it was still double the rate for the white population. Urban areas may provide more jobs, but they also involve costs in terms of leaving behind friends, family, and a familiar culture.

In 1980, 25 percent of white men were employed in high-paying professional and technical jobs, while only 15 percent of Indian men held such jobs. The gap between Indian and white women is nearly as large, and statistics show that Indian women are more concentrated in menial jobs, with about 25 percent employed in such service jobs as motel maids or waitresses.

Many Indians continue to practice their traditional tribal culture, but few are able to support themselves in a traditional way. Hunting, fishing, and gardening are important, especially for reservation Indians. However, Indians rely on cash for certain goods and services and must work to earn income. American Indians who earn their living as hunting and fishing guides, or artists who make pottery, jewelry, or rugs are the exception. Less than 10 percent of American Indians living on reservations in 1980 had these kinds of jobs. In urban areas, this figure is much smaller.

More American Indians are employed in the fields of agriculture, forestry, or mining than whites or African-Americans. Construction companies are an important source of jobs for Indian men, but more Indian men work in manufacturing than in any other type of job.

Federal and tribal governments employ many Native Americans. The federal government continues to have a significant role in day-to-day reservation affairs, and this requires a substantial number of workers. The Bureau of Indian Affairs and the Indian Health Service employ many Native people in jobs such as law enforcement, road construction, logging, health care, law, and real estate. Tribal governments offer jobs in tourism, manufacturing, and other businesses.

In 1980, 17 percent of Indians worked for the federal or state government, compared to only 8 percent of whites. This indicates that there are relatively few opportunities for Indians in private business or industry. Unfortunately, these jobs are often insecure. Funding can be cut at any time, depending on the politics of the federal government, leaving workers jobless.

American Indian Women in the Workforce

Indian women face special problems in finding work. This is especially true in rural areas, where the few jobs available may be in logging or fishing, jobs that are usually held by men. Like many American women, Indian women may also have family obliga-

Bernice Bigman, auditor, makes the final audit of a finished electrical harness before shipment.

tions that limit their ability to work. However, fewer American Indian women work than do women of other races. This may be because they tend to have more children than either white or African-American women do. Indian women with less education tend to have more children and are less likely to work than Indian women with more education.

U.S. Government Assistance to American Indians

For the Navajo and many other tribes who were forced to live on reservations, the first federal assistance was food supplied by soldiers. The Navajo, who were imprisoned at Fort Sumner between 1864 and 1868, were given rotten meat, coffee, tea, sugar, lard, and vermin-infested white flour. These foods, unknown to Indians, were certainly different from the native plants, seeds, nuts, fruits, and wild animals that they were used to eating.

As early as 1883, the Indian agent assigned to the Navajo reservation told the government that it would not be possible for 500 white Americans to make a decent living on the reservation land, even if they used modern technology. At that time, there were 17,000 Navajo living on the reservation! Natural disasters, such as the water shortage of the 1800s in Arizona, did not help matters. Nor did the Great Depression of the 1930s. These disasters take the greatest toll on reservations, where money and resources are already scarce.

Unemployment is high in every Indian community. In some tribes, the majority of members live on unearned income—income from lease payments, pensions, or government assistance. For example, in the late 1960s, 61 percent of the Oglala Sioux tribe in South Dakota received some unearned income. A full 40 percent received only unearned income, and 14 percent had no source of income at all.

Red Cloud, an Oglala Sioux leader, once said that since the resources Native peoples used to live on were taken away by the government, the government owes them a living:

Father, the Great Spirit, did not make us to work. He made us to hunt and fish. He gave us the great prairies and hills and covered them with buffalo, deer, and antelope. He filled the rivers and streams with fish. The white man can work if he wants to, but the Great Spirit did not make us for work. The White man owes us a living for the lands he has taken from us.

In the 1800s and early 1900s, most assistance to the poor was given by private agencies. It was not until the Depression of the 1930s that the U.S. government assumed a central role in caring for the poor and disabled. The idea that the government was responsible for providing a minimum standard of living for everyone was a new concept to the U.S. public, although this idea had been common in most American Indian tribes for centuries.

Indians were not served by local and state programs, and many were excluded even from Social Security and other federal programs. Tribes had to fight throughout the 1940s to be included in these programs. In the late 1940s, an estimated 10,000 Indian families were eligible for assistance, but could not get accepted for benefits. States felt that they were not responsible for American Indians, even though over 75 percent of the money spent by the states came from the federal government. For this reason, the Bureau of Indian Affairs created its own assistance program.

In 1944, a Navajo social worker studied 100 families on 5 different reservations. Of these 100, 91 were living below an acceptable standard of living. Yet the assistance they received was very low—less than $20 a month. In the 1950s, Congress acted to extend Social Security benefits to tribal members by paying states more for the support of Indians than for other groups.

In the 1960s, health programs (Medicare

Indians protesting discrimination in hiring at the Bureau of Indian Affairs office in Denver, Colorado, 1970.

and Medicaid) and social services were added to the Social Security Act. Although the federal government provided greatly needed help, the impact was not as positive as it might have been. In part, this was a result of the programs not being designed or controlled by the tribes. Some of the programs actually conflicted with the community's way of life or set of values to the extent that members were unable to participate. For example, a family may receive food stamps, but have no way to get to a supermarket that will accept food stamps in exchange for food.

In 1975, the Indian Self-Determination and Education Assistance Act was passed. This act encouraged the tribes to administer programs that were formerly run by the Bureau of Indian Affairs. This has become a staggering job because of the many different agencies that the tribes must deal with. Eleven federal departments, the Bureau of Indian Affairs, and a number of other agencies all provide services for Indian peoples.

Altogether, these bureaus and agencies offer hundreds of different programs.

The massive number of programs can be deceiving, however. Not all of the programs that exist on paper are actually funded (have money to operate with). Even after federal and state programs were made available to Indian families, they still receive less aid than non-Indian families. Overall, the average income for Indian families remains lower than that of other groups, including other minority groups. Unemployment rates are higher; living standards, sanitation, and life expectancy are all lower.

Although government agencies are willing to provide aid to tribal communities, they have thus far proved unable to create major development programs that lead to independence.

Aboriginal Economics in Canada

History before European Contact

Pre-contact aboriginal peoples in what is now Canada, as in the United States, had many different kinds of economic systems, usually depending on what resources their environment offered. The sea coast peoples of British Columbia, the northern Arctic peoples, and the Atlantic east coast nations used the abundant products of the sea as the basis of their economies. Their life was generally easier than that of the peoples of the interior plains, whose environment was harsher and less productive. Throughout Canada, complex and sophisticated social, economic, religious, and political institutions developed in accord with the environment.

The Woodlands people, in the large forested lands of central Canada, used the canoe for transportation and raised crops. The Plains people of the great western prairie lands traveled on foot and used dog **travois** (a hauling vehicle made of two long poles that bore a platform or net to carry loads). Technology included the spear, hook, bow and arrow, snare, and buffalo jumps. Shelter was easily constructed out of trees or hides. Social groups varied from the large one-house villages of the Eastern Iroquois to plains buffalo camps, which were small wandering bands of less than one hundred members.

The great Iroquois Confederacy, composed of the Cayuga, Mohawk, Oneida, and Seneca, had an economy based on raising crops of corn, squash, beans, and tobacco in southeastern Ontario and upstate New York. They traded surplus food to neighboring tribes. Seasonal activities included fishing, hunting, preparing fields, planting, harvesting, trading, gathering wild crops and firewood, socializing, making new articles, and conducting ceremonies.

There were many hunting and gathering groups throughout Canada. These groups lived in the forest belts, parklands, and prairies, and had a great diversity of cultural and environmental traits. Economies of these groups revolved around seasonal community management of their resources.

History of Trade with Europeans

Long before Europeans arrived in North America, aboriginal (Native) people traded goods with each other. When the European traders arrived on the continent, they found Native peoples who were generally eager to expand their trade networks with the goods of the newcomers. In the 1600s, First Nations participated fully in the fur trade, exchanging furs and skins for guns, metal tools, cloth, and other European manufactured goods. Manufactured goods obtained from trade with Europeans gradually became a very important part of Native economies in Canada.

For many years, Native peoples have been portrayed as "dupes" who were easily bought off with gaudy trinkets and cheap merchandise. Many historians have shown this to be untrue. First Nations did not join into the fur trade like European consumers. They selected carefully from the goods made available to them and did not simply take whatever European goods were presented. Since they were not conditioned to think of profit just for profit's sake, they often did not trade any more furs than what was needed to supply them with their usual economic needs. With a long history of careful resource management and a community-based distribution of goods, many First Nations were not initially susceptible to the supply and demand market.

This did not suit the European traders, who sought to profit from the great demand for fur in their home countries. In order to obtain more fur from the Native groups, they introduced new trading goods, principally alcohol and tobacco. Eventually pressure from the traders and between Native groups, who often competed for control of trade routes and trapping grounds, resulted in depleting the animal resources in southern Canada. The fur trade then pushed north and west.

Canadian Indians signed a series of "peace and friendship" treaties with the European newcomers starting with the French in the early sixteenth century during the settlement of New France. A trade ceremony often accompanied the signing of the treaty, in which the French trader presented a gift of tea, tobacco, or alcohol to the head man. Colorful cloth was often given to the women, and candy to the children. A lengthy discussion and haggling over the value of the furs and trade goods followed. Sometimes these discussions lasted for several days. After business was completed, parting gifts would be exchanged to confirm the bonds of friendship. A spirit of cooperation and mutual benefit was the basis of this relationship. These early ceremonies and rituals were later adopted for treaty negotiations.

Between 1850 and 1923, 12 treaties were signed by the First Nations and the Canadian government. Unfortunately, the colonial government and the Natives held different views about the sharing of one very important resource—the land. Much misunderstanding between the two groups existed when these treaties were signed. The Canadian government thought it was gaining ownership of lands. For Natives, land could neither be bought nor sold; resources were provided by nature for all people to share for their survival. Most Native groups regarded treaties as promises to keep the peace and share the bountiful resources of the land.

Soon after the first 12 treaties were signed in the late 1800s, the traditional economy of Indian Nations was wiped out when the great bison herds were completely destroyed. Indian treaty negotiators tried to secure the economic future of their people by asking for guarantees that they could continue their hunting and trapping econo-

Noel Nadli checking the fish nets, Point Providence, 1984.

my, but the government insisted on keeping its power to regulate hunting and trapping.

In the mid-1800s, the fur trade declined in southern Canada, although it continued in northern areas until after World War II, or the 1940s. First Nations people responded to this change by adopting various commercial activities. On the prairies, they began to concentrate on farming, although government policies prevented them from participating fully in Canadian markets. In British Columbia, fishing, whaling, and sealing were important. Some coastal peoples worked on farms or in logging camps. In the Arctic the Inuit engaged in whaling and adapting new technologies such as motor

boats and motorized sleds. In the Maritime provinces, however, problems emerged quickly because Native people were denied control over their land and resources. The Micmac, for example, were limited to casual labor, harvesting, or making crafts.

As Canadian industry began to develop in the 1800s, Native people in most parts of the country continued their traditional economic activities. In northern areas, however, the discovery of mineral resources and timber stands brought developments that disrupted Native economies. In some cases, Natives found work with construction crews or in logging camps. They preferred to work at these jobs only at times of the year when they were not busy with hunting, fishing, or other traditional activities.

Overall, Natives were left outside the new industrial economy. Europeans failed to understand the value of traditional ways and simply assumed that Native people were somehow unsuited to work. They argued that Indians were too used to sharing with their communities and did not have enough competitive spirit to succeed in a **capitalist** economy. In many cases, Indians were purposely excluded from participating in the new economic order. Racial discrimination was common, and very few Native people found work in the factories or mining and lumbering operations springing up across Canada.

Over time, the very skills that had made Native peoples so valuable earlier to the fur trade, fishing, and whaling were now devalued. In fact, their skills had been essential to the survival and growth of the European settlements. However, from the mid-1800s to the mid-1900s, First Nations had been made irrelevant to the Canadian economy. Warfare, epidemics, the depletion of game, alcohol, and dependence on manufactured trade goods combined to drastically change Native cultures. The leadership, ceremonial practices, and oral history lost in the epidemics could never be regained. Isolated on reserves, denied access to jobs, and forced to send their children to schools whose main goal was to destroy their culture, Native peoples were soon reduced to poverty and despair.

In the early 1800s, one trader observed:

The native population has decreased at an extraordinary rate.... the natives are no longer the manly, independent race they formerly were. On the contrary, we find them gloomy, dispirited, unhappy and discontented. While resources of the country are thus becoming yearly more and more exhausted, the question naturally suggests itself, what is to become of the natives when their lands can no longer furnish the means of subsistence?

The end result of contact with Europeans was economic dependency and lack of resources with which to begin anew. Government aid and social assistance became a common way of life, beginning in the late 1800s. The government passed the Indian Act in 1876, whose purpose was to manage the affairs of the Indians until they became "civilized." The local Indian agent assigned to manage the reserve controlled every aspect of Native life. Later the "pass system" was begun in order to control Native movement off the reserve. Natives actually had to get a letter of permission to leave! Government policy was aimed at breaking down the Indian culture through control and educating Indians in the ways of mainstream Canadian society.

After World War I, Native organizations were formed across Canada, including the League of Indian Nations. Native leaders began to question government policies and management of Native affairs. High unemployment, short life expectancy, high infant mortality, poverty, poor housing, and open discrimination became issues that were hotly debated. There were calls for justice for Canada's First Nations.

The Indian Act was revised in 1951, but the extensive changes left in place one important fact: the government still had final authority over Native affairs. During the 1960s, the Red Power movement raised the profile of Native issues across North America. [Also see Activism chapter.] It had become apparent that little had changed since reserves were first established. Not only were living conditions terrible for Natives, but they were even denied the tools to effect change. Few Indians could get personal or business loans, and credit was very limited. Native people could not even vote in federal elections until 1960, when the Canadian Bill of Rights was passed!

A push for change resulted during the 1960s and 1970s. During the 1960s, Indian leaders demanded more control over their own affairs, and public support of the issue forced the government to respond. Government programs were created to support Native economic growth and the development of businesses. In general, however, there were few long-term successes. Many programs were short-term efforts aimed at stopping public demand for action. Most were tangled in bureaucratic red tape, which made them ineffective.

During the 1970s, Native leadership such as the National Indian Brotherhood called for transfer of control of Native peoples' affairs to local communities. They wanted development efforts to be managed by those who would benefit. Indians wanted to define their own problems, find solutions, and develop programs and enterprises that would incorporate their own social, cultural, educational, and political systems. Self-determination came to be seen as the key factor in promoting lasting economic success for Native peoples.

Community development at the grass-roots level is a popular method that offers hope for the future. A main goal of commu-nity development is to create jobs on the reserves for band members. Another is to take control of economic development to ensure that the land and its natural resources are managed to benefit the reserve. A key factor in deciding which projects to pursue and how to manage them is whether the community and its members will be able to maintain their special cultures and traditions, and whether the project will promote Native self-esteem, pride, and values. Projects will be judged by whether or not they protect land ownership and respect the sacredness of the land and environment.

In recent years, many Native communities have begun to change. They are preparing long-range plans, setting down goals, and creating a vision for the future. Canada's Native peoples have gained recognition in the Constitution for "the inherent right to self-government" as a "third order government." This means that the First Nations are equal in stature to the federal and provincial governments. Restrictions still imposed by the Indian Act are under review. In the words of Calvin Helin, a columnist for the Native Voice, and president of the Native Investment and Trade association:

> The emerging new era of Canada's First People towards socio-economic self-reliance will bring about unprecedented opportunities in the development and utilization of vast resources in land, capital—and people. The challenge in this quest for self-reliance is to build bridges to the private sector, fundamental in the development of First Nations' economies. Joint ventures and the exploration of related

business opportunities for native and non-native enterprise simply makes good business sense.

Aboriginal Businesses

The recent establishment of Native enterprises points to a major problem. A journalist once described the efforts of blacks to create businesses in South Africa as being like asking people to join a Monopoly game three hours after the game started, when all the best properties and utilities had already been bought. Native peoples are entering late in the game as well.

Another barrier lies in the conflict between the communal values of the Native culture and the demands of capitalism to be competitive and look for personal gain. Native people who succeed in business but ignore community obligations may have to pay large social and personal costs—loss of friendships or status among the community, for example. On the other hand, people who put community needs ahead of sound business practices may fit in with society, but may soon be out of business.

In spite of these constraints, many Native businesses have emerged across Canada. Natives own and operate retail stores, video stores, gas stations, hotels, publishing companies, radio stations, and construction companies. Natives are commercial artists, and commercial fishermen and trappers. Others operate trailer parks in urban areas, or rent reserve land for other commercial ventures. However, these businesses are far from common. A number of Native businesses are dependent on government support even after many years of operation. Also, recessions often hit these businesses harder, causing failures.

Perhaps the greatest commercial success was created by the Inuit in the eastern Arctic in the late 1950s. The Inuit originated the **cooperative** movement. Cooperatives hire and train Native workers whenever possible, and keep profits within the community. Participation in the Inuit cooperatives provided a training ground for many leaders who went on to hold positions in government, politics, or other areas.

The cooperatives began with retail stores and the commercial development of arts and crafts, especially carving and print-making. The cooperatives distributed Inuit art nationally and internationally, and soon Inuit arts and crafts became widely known and valued. And importantly, they began to command high prices. By the 1970s, the cooperatives organized into the Arctic Cooperatives and expanded into hotels, tourism, the fur trade, transportation, and other services.

There have been no similar large-scale successes with cooperative enterprises in other parts of Canada. However, Native people have ventured into a number of different areas with some success, providing optimism for future successes. Native people remain involved in development of resources such as furs, fishing, timber, oil, and minerals. Road construction, commercial art and handicrafts, retail stores, and tourism are other areas in which Native people are active. The Inuit, for example, have sold packaged tours based in Native communities that have brought hundreds of tourists into the Arctic. A Native-run cooperative, Yukon Native Products, has combined the traditional with the modern; they sell traditional handicrafts, but also run a factory to make parkas.

There have been a number of well-known success stories in First Nation business and community development. For example, the Cree in James Bay settled their land claims in the 1970s, and used the money to move in a dramatic fashion. Led by Chief Billy Diamond, they purchased an airline and named it AirCreebec. They attracted the business of a Japanese company, which resulted in the building of a canoe factory. An innovative project in Paddle Prairie, Alberta, shows that creativity can solve the problem of fitting capitalist and community values. There the gas station and retail store are community-owned. In other words, local people own shares in the stores and distribute profits among themselves, while the managers have the freedom to run the business.

The Sechelt band in British Columbia has devised another novel approach. Instead of developing business in order to provide jobs, they focus on developing business in order to gain profits for the community—regardless of whether or not Natives are employed.

A gravel pit operation, for example, employs a number of non-Natives and still provides significant money for the band.

There is no simple model for Native businesses, and there is no one right way to develop enterprises. There are also no certainties in business. On the positive side, land claims settlements often provide large sums of cash that allow Native bands to enter the marketplace. Self-government has removed some of the barriers to business success that have plagued Indians through the past centuries. At the same time, economic recessions and cuts in government funding put pressure on Native business efforts.

Many leaders remain hopeful, however. They see commercial success as a way to break the cycle of poverty and despair that has gripped their communities for so long. Effort and resources are being poured into establishing these businesses, as Native people struggle to overcome their economic problems and gain greater control over their future.

17
Native North American Languages

FACT FOCUS

- The state of California has more language families than all of Europe.
- Half of the names of states in the United States were borrowed from Native American languages.
- It is predicted that by the year 2050, only a dozen of the original three hundred Native American languages will still be actively spoken.
- The Navajo language is spoken by about one hundred thousand people.
- Sign language was used among tribes of the Great Plains, who spoke many different languages. Sign language consisted mainly of gestures, but sometimes included the use of smoke, mirrors, or blankets, enabling Plains people to communicate across large areas.

Originally there may have been as many as three hundred Native North American languages. Unfortunately, many have become extinct because of contact with Europeans. For a number of reasons, over the years Native American groups have gradually replaced their tribal languages with English, French, or Spanish. At the present time, however, over one hundred Native American languages may still be spoken. The number of people who speak these languages varies greatly. Navajo, for example, is spoken by about one hundred thousand people and is still learned by many children as their first language. Other languages are remembered by only a few elders.

Native North American languages are spoken by Native peoples in the continental United States and Canada. However, some of these languages are also spoken in other places. For example, Inuit (an Eskimo language) is the principal language of Greenland. Also, several languages native to the southwestern United States are spoken in Mexico and Central America.

Why Study Native American Languages?

American Indian languages are studied for several reasons. One very important reason is that so many of them are becoming extinct. People interested in preserving Native American cultures want to learn them from the last speakers of these languages. However, although many languages have been lost, not all Native American languages face extinction. Many Native Americans today take a strong interest in maintaining the use of their languages as a way of preserving tribal identity and traditions.

Understanding even those languages that are becoming extinct and have never been put into writing can add to our understanding of American history. Although we often think of history as something that was recorded in writing, our knowledge of history can come from a number of different sources. Often languages are studied along with archeological finds and native traditions. In this way, much can be learned about prehistoric homelands, how tribes moved from one area to another (migrations), and who they came into contact with.

Language Families

Many scientists and historians believe that during the last Ice Age, over 25,000 years ago, Asia and America were linked by a bridge of land. This land bridge, called Beringia, was located where the Bering Strait is now. Different groups of people from Asia crossed over into present-day Alaska and Canada. These peoples spoke several different languages, many of which are no longer spoken in Asia today. Over time, tribes migrated south into Canada and the United States. Their languages changed and developed into many different languages.

North American Indian languages are very **diverse,** or different from each other. No single set of characteristics is shared by all of them. Still, they can be grouped into 57 families. A family is a group of languages that

are related. There are more **language families** in the western part of the continent than in the East, with 37 families west of the Rockies. California alone has 20, which shows more variety than in all of Europe.

Parent and Sister Languages

Even though they are different, many Native American languages are related. They may share similar words, sounds, or structures (the way words are put together). This may have happened in two ways. The languages may have borrowed from each other, or they may have developed from a common origin (from a **parent language**).

A group of languages that has come from one parent are called **sister languages.** Sister languages all belong to one language family. They share many similar words. For example, the word *cow* is written *vacca* in Italian, *vaca* in Spanish, and *vache* in French. These are all Romance languages (meaning they came from Latin). Such sets of words are also found among American Indian languages. For example, the word *chief* is *okimaawa* in Fox, *okimaaw* in Cree, *okeemaaw* in Menominee, and *okimaa* in Ojibway. All these are sister languages in the Algonkian family.

However, we can never be absolutely sure that languages are similar only because they came from the same parent language. Languages can also borrow words from each other. This may have happened long ago among the parent languages. Borrowing words, sounds, and language structures continues even today.

Language Contact and Borrowing

North American Indian languages have always been in contact with each other.

Tribes learned the languages of other groups when they needed to communicate. Perhaps they wished to trade, to talk about a problem, or just to know each other. In some tribes, people spoke two or more languages. This resulted in borrowing among languages.

Words that languages borrow from each other are often called **loan words.** Grammar, punctuation, and language structure might also be shared. People who study Native American languages have divided the North American continent into language areas. These are geographical areas where languages have many of the same features. Examples of language areas are the Arctic and Northeast.

Some tribes developed a **lingua franca**, or trade language, in order to communicate with each other. When European settlers arrived they learned these trade languages and added new words of their own. A good example is Chinook Jargon, spoken in the Pacific Northwest. Chinook Jargon added many French and English words. Some Chinook Jargon loan words are *kosho,* which comes from the French *cochon* (pig), and *lapush,* from the French *la bouche* (mouth).

Russian words have entered native languages in Alaska, and Spanish has been borrowed in the southwestern United States. The amount of borrowing varies greatly. For example, after several centuries of contact with the Spanish, the Navajo language has borrowed almost no loan words. Pueblo has borrowed a few, and O'Odham has used a very large number.

The Plains Sign Language is a special kind of lingua franca. It is a language of gestures used among tribes of the Great Plains and later learned by many whites. The Plains

WORDS TO KNOW

bilingual: speaking two languages fluently.

diverse: things or people that are different from one another.

language family: a group of languages that are different from one another but are related. These languages share similar words, sounds, or word structures. The languages are similar either because they have borrowed words from each other or because they originally came from the same parent language.

loan words: words that people who speak one language have taken or "borrowed" from another language.

lingua franca: a language that is created so that people who speak different languages can communicate well enough to trade with each other.

parent language: a language that is the common source of two or more languages that came into being at a later time.

pictographs: simple pictures drawn on skin, wood, or other surfaces to represent events, ideas, or other meanings.

sister languages: languages that stem from a common source, the parent language. Sister languages usually differ from each other because they developed in a different area, but they retain some or many similarities.

syllabary: a system of writing that uses characters (letters) to represent whole syllables (rather than letters representing consonants and vowels, as in an alphabet system).

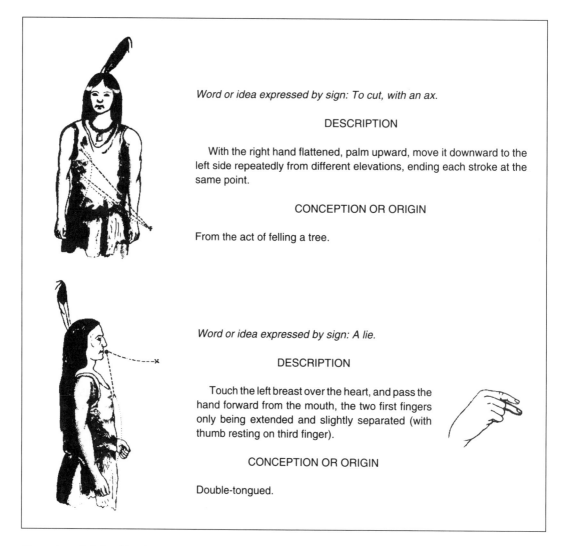

Word or idea expressed by sign: To cut, with an ax.

DESCRIPTION

With the right hand flattened, palm upward, move it downward to the left side repeatedly from different elevations, ending each stroke at the same point.

CONCEPTION OR ORIGIN

From the act of felling a tree.

Word or idea expressed by sign: A lie.

DESCRIPTION

Touch the left breast over the heart, and pass the hand forward from the mouth, the two first fingers only being extended and slightly separated (with thumb resting on third finger).

CONCEPTION OR ORIGIN

Double-tongued.

Examples of Plains Sign Language

tribes spoke many different languages, but since they moved around a lot there was not enough contact to encourage borrowing. Their system of signs and gestures was especially useful on the Plains, where people could see for great distances. Sign language, which sometimes included the use of smoke, mirrors, or blankets, enabled Plains people to communicate across large areas without having to travel toward each other.

In a few areas, languages have been mixed as a result of tribal contact. New languages have been created that clearly don't belong to the family of either parent. The best-known example of this is Michif or Metchif, currently spoken in North Dakota.

NATIVE WORDS BORROWED INTO ENGLISH, AND THE EARLIEST KNOWN DATES OF BORROWING

Animal Names:	Plant Names:	Cultural Features:
Caribou, 1610	Persimmon, 1612	Totem, 1609
Opossum, 1610	Hickory, 1629	Moccasin, 1612
Moose, 1613	Squash, 1643	Tomahawk, 1612
Skunk, 1634	Pecan, 1778	Powwow, 1624
Terrapin, 1672	Tamarack, 1805	Wigwam, 1628
Woodchuck, 1674		Manitou (a deity), 1671
Quahog (clam), 1799		Toboggan, 1829
Chipmunk, 1841		

The Karuk of northwestern California are a tribe who suffered very harsh treatment at the hands of white people. As a result, their language shows very few loan words. Languages that do not borrow often create new vocabulary by combining native words in a new way. For example, the Karuk word for *hotel* is *am-naam,* which means "eating-place."

Native Words Borrowed into English

Of course, borrowing also occurs in the other direction. Many Native American words have been borrowed into English and other European languages. The oldest known loan into English is *raccoon,* from an Algonkian language. *Raccoon* occurs in a letter written by Captain John Smith from Virginia in 1608. This was quickly followed by many other borrowings from Algonkian, as Europeans made contact with tribes along the Atlantic seacoast.

As Europeans moved westward across the continent, they borrowed words from other language families. *Teepee,* for example, came from Siouan. More recent loan words from the far West are *hooch* (illegal liquor) from the Tlingit of Alaska, and *abalone* (a shellfish) from Costanoan in California. In addition, English adopted many words from Spanish that originally came from Indian languages. Examples are *maize, potato,* and *barbeque* from the West Indies; and *tomato, chili,* and *coyote* from the Aztecs in Mexico.

Many place names have been borrowed from Native American languages. In fact, half of our state names come from Native American languages. Although most place names were borrowed from tribes that lived in the same area, there are some interesting exceptions. For example, the name *Wyoming* was borrowed from a place name in Pennsylvania. It was originally an Algonkian word. The name *Sequoia,* given to the famous California trees and park, was not local either. It was borrowed from Sequoyah, who invented the Cherokee writing system and lived in present-day Arkansas.

Listed below are more examples of place names that Americans borrowed from Native peoples:

Algonkian names in the northeastern and central states:
Connecticut, Ottawa, Manhattan, Potomac, Allegheny, Illinois, Michigan, Wisconsin, Chicago, Mississippi (meaning "big water"), Manitoba, and Saskatchewan.

Iroquoian names in the Great Lakes and the South:
Ticonderoga, Conestoga, Niagara, Chautauqua, Ohio, Kentucky, and Tennessee.

Siouan place names in the Midwest:
Iowa, Missouri, Arkansas, Kansas, Nebraska, Minnesota, and Dakota.

Muskogean names in the South:
Alabama, Appalachia, and Oklahoma.

Place names from the languages of the far West:

Arizona and Tucson (both from Pima-Papago), Utah (from Ute), Seattle (from the name of a Salishan chief in the Puget Sound area), and Alaska (from Aleut).

Geographical and Language Areas

There are 11 geographical areas in North America where Native American culture and physical environment are very similar. In some of these areas, such as the Northwest, languages are closely related. In others areas, like the Plains, the languages remain very different.

These areas can be arranged into four different groups:

1) **The Arctic, Western Subarctic, Eastern Subarctic, and Great Basin.** In each of these areas, languages came from a common origin but very little borrowing occurred. Most likely, this happened because tribes did not live close to each other. In other words, low population density resulted in very little sharing of language.

2) **California, the Southwest, Northwest, Northeast, and Southeast.** Here languages have many different origins. Borrowing has been local only (between neighboring tribes) and has not resulted in widespread sharing. This may have resulted from low population density. These groups share location and culture, but the languages remain different.

3) **The Plains.** In this area languages came from many sources, but borrowing has been very limited. There may be two reasons for this: a) Plains people have lived in this area for a relatively short period of time; and b) The Plains Sign Language has enabled the tribes to communicate without verbal language.

4) **The Northwest and Plateau.** Here languages came from different sources but show a great deal of similarity. High population density (tribes located close to each other) probably encour-

aged borrowing. Also, the cultures may have valued social or other contacts between members of tribes.

Language and Culture

There are many striking differences between Native American and European languages. This has led to the question: Are the languages different because the cultures are so different? People may have developed different ways of expressing themselves because they have very different ideas about the world and their places in it. Or could it be that the language people learn as children shapes the way they think?

For example, Europeans use *north, south, east,* and *west* to indicate direction. These directions relate to the sun. The Karuk and others in California use terms like *upriver, downriver, away from the river, uphill,* and *toward the river, downhill.* The Karuk define direction in relation to the Klamath River, which winds through their territory.

Another way languages may differ greatly is in words used for relatives. For example, English has one word for *uncle.* The Seneca language has two—one for the father's brother (*ha'nih*), and a different one for the mother's brother (*hakhno'senh*). Perhaps in the Seneca culture the two types of uncles play different roles or have a different status. Therefore, they need to have separate names.

Languages also count differently. English and many European languages have a counting system based on the number ten. Thirteen, for example, was originally "three [plus] ten," while thirty was "three [times] ten." This clearly reflects that a person's ten fingers were used to help in counting long ago when the system was started.

In many Native American Indian languages, the number five (representing the fingers of one hand) or the number twenty (the fingers plus the toes) may be used as basic units. For example, in the Luiseno language in California, six was called "five adding one"; ten was "both my hands finished"; fifteen was "both my hands finished and one of my feet"; and twenty was "my other foot finished also."

Many Native American societies, such as the Navajo, have no name for their tribe or language. They simply call themselves "the people" and their language is called "the language of the people." However, other tribes do have names for themselves. For instance, the Hopi call themselves *hopi.*

In any part of the world, the number of words people use to describe something shows how important that object is to them. For example, the Inuit (Eskimo) have four words for snow: "falling snow," "snow on the ground," and two types of "drifting snow." As a matter of fact, one might say that English has at least four words for snow. We have words like "slush," "sleet," and "blizzard." After all, snow is also important in many parts of the English-speaking world!

Another interesting question is whether the languages people learn as children cause them to think in certain ways. For example, the Hopi word for *day* has no plural form and can't be counted the way English speakers count "three days." Instead the Hopi might say "first day," or "second day." Some people believe this is because the Hopi don't think of each day as unique or different. They view each day as part of a cycle of

Cherokee Alphabet

D a	R e	T i	Ꭳ o	Ꝏ u	i v
S ga Ꝃ ka	Ꝑ ge	Ꝩ gi	A go	J gu	E gv
Ꮤ ha	Ꝑ he	Ꭷ hi	Ꝉ ho	Ꝅ hu	Ꝋ hv
W la	Ꮣ le	Ꮅ li	G lo	M lu	Ꮑ lv
Ꮆ ma	Ꮉ me	H mi	Ꮽ mo	Ꮎ mu	
Ꝋ na Ꮏ hna Ꮐ nah	Λ ne	ꭾ ni	Z no	Ꝩ nu	Ꝋ nv
Ꮖ qua	Ꮗ que	Ꮔ qui	Ꮝ quo	Ꮗ quu	Ꮨ quv
Ꮖ sa Ꮝ s	Ꮞ se	Ꮢ si	Ꮧ so	Ꮡ su	R sv
Ꮣ da Ꮤ ta	Ꮪ de Ꮤ te	Ꮧ di Ꮨ ti	Ꮩ do	Ꮪ du	Ꮫ dv
Ꮬ dla Ꮅ tla	Ꮮ tle	Ꮣ tli	Ꮯ tlo	Ꮰ tlu	Ꮲ tlv
Ꮳ tsa	Ꮴ tse	Ꮵ tsi	Ꮶ tso	Ꮷ tsu	Ꮸ tsv
Ꮹ wa	Ꮺ we	Ꮻ wi	Ꮼ wo	Ꮽ wu	Ꮾ wv
Ꮿ ya	Ᏸ ye	Ᏹ yi	Ᏺ yo	Ᏻ yu	Ᏼ yv

Sounds Represented by Vowels

a, as a in father, or short as a in rival

e, as a in hate, or short as e in met

i, as i in pique, or short as i in pit

o, as o in note, approaching aw in law

u, as oo in fool, or short as u in pull

v, as u in but, nasalized

Consonant Sounds

g nearly as in English, but approaching to k. d nearly as in English but approaching to t. h k l m n q s t w y as in English. Syllables beginning with g except S (ga) have sometimes the power of k. A (go), S (du), Ꮫ (dv) are sometimes sounded to, tu, tv and syllables written with tl except Ꮅ (tla) sometimes vary to dl.

Cherokee Syllabary. From *Beginning Cherokee,* by Ruth Bradley Holmes and Betty Sharp Smith, 2d ed.

Syllabary:	WℙᎯ　Ｇℇℽ　Ꭿℰℐℭℸ
Pronunciation:	Ta?-li:ˈ-ne Tsa-la-giˈ Go-hwe-lv:ˈ-i
Translation:	Second Cherokee Lesson

Example of Cherokee in Sequoyah's syllabary, in phonetic transcription, and in translation. From *Beginning Cherokee*, by Ruth Bradley Holmes and Betty Sharp Smith, 2nd ed.

time, with many activities and ceremonies being repeated each day. Therefore they see tomorrow more or less as a repeat of today.

Often, language can tell us something about the history of a culture and how people came to live in an area. For example, the Athapaskan languages of the Southwest probably originated in the Subarctic. To support this idea, we can trace changes in language. Sometimes a single word can have two different meanings. In Athapaskan language in the far north a single word meaning *horn* or *spoon* was used, because spoons were made of deerhorn. As these peoples moved south and settled in the southwestern United States, that same word came to mean *gourd* or *spoon,* because spoons were made of gourds.

Writing Systems

Before the arrival of Europeans, some American Indian groups used **pictographs** to record their history. Pictographs are simple pictures drawn on skin or wood to represent events, ideas, or other meanings. These are not accurate in the way that written language is, because people can read different meanings into the same pictograph.

Various types of writing have also been used by Native American tribes. Early in the settlement of New England, the European alphabet was adapted to write the Massachusett language. The Micmac of Nova Scotia adopted a hieroglyphic system (a system of writing that uses pictures rather than an alphabet) in the nineteenth century. However, this system proved too difficult to use, and in recent years they changed to an alphabetic system.

The most famous Native American writing system was invented for the Cherokee in about 1820. Sequoyah, who was half Cherokee, knew no English but he had seen materials written in English. He decided to invent a writing system for the Cherokee language.

Sequoyah's system is called a **syllabary.** While an alphabet system like the one used in English uses letters to form sounds that combine to make up syllables, a syllabary system uses characters (or letters) to form whole syllables. Sequoyah borrowed some of the letter shapes from the English alphabet, but did not give them the same sounds. For example, the Cherokee *D* is pronounced like an *a* and *R is* pronounced like an *e.*

Alphabets are used for most other Native

The Inuit people of the Arctic try to preserve their language by providing reading material in Inuit for their young people.

American writing. When necessary, additional letters and accent marks are added to represent sounds not found in English. In most cases the English alphabet is used, although the Aleuts adapted the Russian alphabet.

Some Native Americans distrust writing systems and prefer to continue oral traditions. In 1991, the president of the Oglala Sioux tribe announced that Lakota would be the language of tribal business on the Pine River Reservation. However, he did not approve of writing the language down. "Writing it is bad," he said, "because you have a tendency to lose some of the spirituality when it's down in black and white." In spite of such feelings, writing may help some tribes to preserve their traditional literature and history.

Preserving Native American Languages

Since their first contact with Europeans, Native Americans have been pressured to learn European languages. In the early to middle 1800s, **bilingualism** (speaking two languages) was common in many Native American communities. English or French were usually necessary for dealing with whites, but native languages were often used in schools, churches, newspapers, and government offices.

The use of two languages began to change in the late 1800s. At that time the United States government decided to stamp out the use of native languages. Many Native Americans were removed from their homes and taken to boarding schools, where they were actually punished for speaking anything other than English!

After the Indian Reorganization Act of 1934, there was some change in official attitudes. Attempts were made to revive Native American languages. However, by this time many Indian parents had already decided that speaking English was best for their children's future. As a result, many Native languages became extinct. Today it is common to find languages that are spoken by only a few of the elders.

Because traditional Native American culture and history have usually been passed on to the young orally, there are often no written records to preserve this knowledge. When a tribe's language becomes extinct, a large piece of its culture and history are lost forever.

Since the 1970s, efforts have been made to bring back or keep traditional languages. Sometimes this is done by teaching reading and writing in native languages. In some groups, children are growing up as active bilinguals. Examples can be found among the Inuit and Cree in Canada, and the Sioux, Cherokee, Navajo, and Pueblos in the United States.

Unfortunately, each new generation of Native Americans knows less of its Native languages than the one before. It has been estimated that by the middle of the next century only a dozen of the original three hundred Native American languages will be actively spoken.

18
Native American Education

FACT FOCUS

- The first school established for Indians by Europeans was founded by the Jesuits (a Catholic religious order) in Havana, Cuba, in 1568, for the purpose of converting Indians to Christianity.
- While most public education was handled by states and local communities, the U.S. federal government controlled the education of Native American children from the 1700s, when the treaties were signed that established reservations and the right of Indians to education, until the early twentieth century.
- Today, about 88 percent of Native American children attend public schools.
- Beginning in 1860, boarding schools, and the separation of Native American children from their families and culture, were the preferred methods of the government for the education of Native American children. By 1892, the government was operating more than one hundred Indian boarding schools, both on and off reservations.
- In 1966, the Navajo tribe created the first college in the U.S. controlled by a Native tribe, the Navajo Community College. There are now 22 tribally controlled colleges in the United States.
- In the seventeenth century French colonists and missionaries in Canada sent Native children with "potential" to France to be educated, with devastating results for the children.
- In Canada, some Indian schools feature a cultural survival camp, where staff and students go to a reserve for one week to live with elders in the traditional way. Elders teach students traditional skills, tell stories and legends, and perform rituals.

"Going to school and getting an education are two different things and they do not always happen at the same time."—Dr. Rosa M. Hill (a Mohawk woman), 1930

Formal education for American Indians and Alaska Natives developed differently than it did for other people in the United States. For Native peoples, education was a right guaranteed by the four hundred treaties they signed with the federal government between 1778 and 1871. These treaties exchanged almost one billion acres of Indian land for services such as health care and education, protection against invasion, and self-government for "as long as the grass grows and the rivers flow."

The Bureau of Indian Affairs (BIA) ran Indian schools for more than one hundred years. During this time, the federal government operated these schools, allowing little or no local control. In contrast, schools for non-Indian children were governed by state governments, local school boards, and parents.

To a very great extent, the federal government looked on Indian schools as a way to **assimilate** Native children into "white" society. The government hoped that education would cause Native American children to abandon their traditions and culture, and eventually become "Americanized." Since this was the main goal of Indian schools, it is not surprising that Indian parents were not allowed to have a voice in their children's education. This would not change until the 1970s.

Informal Education before Columbus and the Colonists

Every human society has a process for teaching youth to adopt its social customs and culture. This process of education prepares young people to participate in society as adults. Before European colonists arrived on the continent, most Native North American children learned by watching and doing. The entire community served as their teachers: parents, older brothers and sisters, relatives, and elders. Through the community

---

WORDS TO KNOW

assimilate: to absorb, or blend into, the culture of another population. For many years, the federally controlled education systems for Native American children encouraged and even enforced the *assimilation* of Native students to European traditions and ways of life.

boarding school: a school where students live all or part of the year.

curriculum: the courses or classes offered in a school.

formal education: structured learning that takes place in a school or college, under the supervision of teachers.

higher education: education at a college, university, or other post-secondary learning institution.

informal education: learning that takes place outside of a school or classroom. Learning through observation, participation, or practice things like how to prepare for a ceremony, make a teepee, or speak a language.

literacy: the state of being able to read and write.

mission school: a school established by missionaries to teach people new religious beliefs, as well as other subjects.

---

the children learned language, customs, traditions, and values—things that were useful and meaningful to them in their way of life. When the children became adults, they were expected to teach the next generation, just as they had been taught.

The boarding schools for Indians sought the complete transformation of the Indians to white ways. This scene from the school of Genoa, Nebraska, sometime around 1910, shows a school band.

Formal Education: Religious, Federal, and Indian

Control of formal education for Indians after European contact has passed through the hands of three groups: first religious groups, then the federal government, and finally to Indian communities. For many years, the main goal of the religious and federal schools was to force Native American children to adopt the dominant American culture. Well into the twentieth century, educators, missionaries, and government policymakers have referred to the process of converting Native Americans to European-based culture as "civilizing" them, although Native cultures already had their own civilizations and ways.

Religious Schools

From the late 1500s to the 1800s, **mission schools** were the main source of formal education for Native peoples. Mission schools were run by religious orders, such as the Jesuits and Franciscans, but were also supported by government funds.

The first school established by Europeans to educate Indians was founded by the Jesuits (a Catholic religious order) in Havana, Cuba, in 1568. The French and Spanish wanted to convert the Indians to Catholicism, so Jesuit and Franciscan missionaries taught Native children mainly about religion.

The English Protestant religious groups also had great influence on Indian education in the early years of their settlement on the North American continent. In the English colonies, schools were run by the church and government together. Reading, writing, arithmetic, religion, and industrial arts were taught. During the colonial period, two people were especially important in determining the future of education for Indians: John Eliot, a Puritan missionary, and Dr. Eleazer Wheelock, headmaster of the Moors Charity School. Both wanted to convert and "civilize" Indians, but they each used different methods to reach their goals.

John Eliot learned the Algonkian dialect and was able to preach sermons directly to the Indians to convince them to give their children a Puritan education. Once they were convinced, Indian people asked for their own schools and governments. Land was purchased and "praying towns" were established where Indian converts could live together with a lifestyle that imitated the colonists. In these Indian "praying towns," attempts to Christianize and educate the Indians in European traditions were quite successful.

Dr. Wheelock's idea was to remove Indian children from their families and tribes. They would be placed in schools and homes where they could be exposed to "civilized" life. Ideally, they would then return to their communities and continue to convert their own people to mainstream American ways and beliefs. Dr. Wheelock's school, Moors Charity School (which later became Dartmouth College), enrolled many Indian students during its early years. In 1775, the Continental Congress gave $500 to educate Indians at Dartmouth.

Federal Boarding Schools

In 1860 the first federal **boarding school**

Group of Omaha boys in cadet uniforms, Carlisle Indian School, Pennsylvania, 1880.

was established on Yakima Indian reservation in Washington. Five years later, the government decided that boarding schools should be located away from Indian communities. It was hoped that by isolating Indian children even further from their families and communities, they would more quickly become Americanized. The first of these off-reservation schools was established in 1879 in Carlisle, Pennsylvania.

The federal boarding schools for Indians were seen as a way to solve the "Indian problem" (the government's way of describing the existence of separate, sovereign Native nations with their own cultures). Cultures, traditions, and languages were to be suppressed (or eliminated) through the re-education of Native children who had been removed from the influences of their families and communities. Native peoples did not easily accept this, but when they refused to send their children to federal boarding schools, more rules regarding attendance were put in place. The government enforced attendance by denying food to families who didn't send their children to school. By this time Indian people on reservations depended almost totally on the government for food rations, so cutting off their supply of food was a powerful tool.

Many Indian students at the federal boarding schools felt lonely and longed to return home, while others adjusted to the new life and returned to the reservations only after they had finished school. Some never did return to the reservations. Because terminating reservations and the sovereign status of Indians was one of the government's goals, each student who failed to return to the reservation was a success story for policymakers. However, the boarding schools were very expensive to run. Also, very few students returned to the reservations in order to influence others to adopt an "American" lifestyle. The widespread conversion that was hoped for did not occur.

Later in the 1800s the policy of moving children off the reservations was changed and more boarding schools were established on reservations. These were less expensive to operate. Also, most Indian parents did not object to the education itself—they just didn't want to lose contact with their children. It was hoped that if the schools were located closer to the families, parents would be more willing to send their children. By 1892, the U.S. government was operating more than one hundred Indian boarding schools, both on and off reservations.

Indian Schools

In the late 1700s, the Cherokee, Chickasaw, Choctaw, Creek, and Seminole nations of the Southeast responded to government interference in the education of their children by developing their own schools. The Cherokee people had developed a syllabary that presented the Cherokee language in print. [Also see Languages chapter.] With their writing system, Cherokee people had a higher **literacy** rate (the percentage of people who could read and write) than the settlers who lived nearby.

The accomplishments of the Southeastern tribes earned them the title of "The Five Civilized Tribes." Despite their achievements, however, these five tribes were forced to leave their homelands in the East and Southeast. In the forced evacuation called the "Trail of Tears," these tribes were cruelly marched on foot in harsh conditions to settle in what is now Oklahoma. Many died during the removal, but in spite of this disruption, the Cherokee reestablished their unique educational system in their new lands. When the state of Oklahoma was created in the early 1900s, the U.S. Congress abolished the Cherokee school system, and Indian control of education was lost once again. Later in the twentieth century many Indian groups established their own community schools, modeled after the school systems of the Five Civilized Tribes.

Public Schools

Federal boarding schools were not effective in changing or eliminating the distinc-

Andi LeBeau and Kirsten Martel enjoy a moment during graduation, 1990.

tive features of Indian ways of life. This became apparent to the government by the early 1900s, and policy was changed to educate Native children in the nation's public schools. At about this time, the Dawes Allotment Act was taking effect, which divided reservation land into parcels that were to be privately owned by individual Native Americans. One of the results of this act was that some parcels of reservation land were sold to non-Indian settlers. Public schools were then needed for the settlers' children as well.

Reforms in Indian Schools

In 1928 the Meriam Report on the education of Native Americans described Indian boarding schools as deplorable. Many problems were found, including widespread illness, poor living conditions, and low teacher salaries. The report also criticized the Uniform Course of Study, which dictated that all Indian children should study the same things at the same time of year. In addition, the skills that were taught often did not prepare students for the job market.

In the 1930s, changes were made. Some of the boarding schools were closed. The Uniform Course of Study was gradually replaced with courses that were related to the cultures and traditions of the Native children. Bilingual books were used, and teachers were given training in order to promote bilingual education. But in the 1940s, World War II took the nation's attention away from school reform. It was not until the 1960s that reform was promoted again. In a message to Congress in 1968, President Lyndon B. Johnson said that it was important for Native Americans to play a greater role in planning and directing community programs, including education.

The Bureau of Indian Affairs began to contract with Indian groups to operate their own schools. Two notable examples are schools on the Navajo reservation: Rough Rock Demonstration School in Arizona and Ramah High School in New Mexico. Ramah High School was the first Indian-controlled high school since the closing of the Cherokee and Choctaw school systems in the early 1900s. At Rough Rock, Navajo was the primary language spoken, with special time spent on learning English. Urban schools, such as the Red School House in St. Paul and the Heart of the Earth Survival School in Minneapolis, were also established. Tribal culture, history, and language were featured in the curricula of these and other urban schools with Native American students.

In 1969, a government report titled "Indian Education: A National Tragedy—A National Challenge," was published. This report called Indian education "disastrous." High absenteeism and drop-out rates, academic failures, and negative self-esteem were cited as problems. The report said that these problems resulted from schooling that failed to understand or adapt to Native American cultures. The report recommended teaching Indian history, culture, and language, and involving Indian parents in the education of their children.

During the 1970s and 1980s, several major pieces of legislation were passed by Congress, and a number of reports were published. All agreed that Native American people should have more control over the education of their children, and that reform efforts should continue. In a way, Native American education had come full circle. Before Europeans came to this country, Native peoples did control the education of their children. Now, after more than five hundred years, there was agreement that this was a good thing!

Since the 1970s, a spirit of Indian self-determination has emerged in the field of education. Native Americans have had increasing influence on programs for their children. Although much remains to be done, there has been remarkable progress, and Indian leaders remain hopeful.

Native American Education Today

The Bureau of Indian Affairs (BIA) funds 182 elementary and secondary schools. Of these, 83 are operated by Native tribes. These BIA-funded schools are located on 63 reservations in 23 different states. The BIA also runs 5 boarding schools located off-reservation. Altogether, more than 40,000 students are served by about 6,000 teachers and support staff.

Only about 7 percent of Indian students in the United States attend BIA schools.

Special programs have been designed to build a modern education system around the values of traditional Indian culture.

Another 5 percent attend private or parochial (church) schools. The remaining 88 percent attend the nation's public schools. As of 1990, about 383,000 Native American or Alaska Native students attended grades kindergarten through 12 in the public schools. Native children represent about 1 percent of the total U.S. student population.

Across the United States, nearly one hundred bilingual programs are operating in schools that have Indian students. One of the main reasons these programs exist is the concern that many Indian languages are dying. With each generation, there are fewer and fewer speakers of these languages.

Rock Point Community School in Arizona is a successful Navajo bilingual school. As one example, Rock Point high school students participate in a Navajo Research Class, researching issues and reporting results in Navajo or English. The reports are then published in their bilingual newspaper.

Most Native American educators agree that language and culture are important and can be included in the **curriculum**. By participating in Native languages and culture classes, Native American children are experiencing a higher level of self-esteem. In addition, the American public's perception of Native peoples is being altered by these

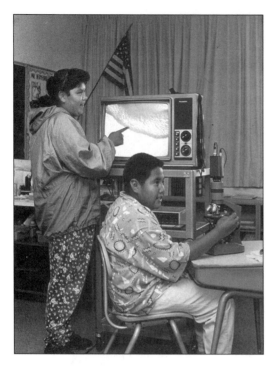

A Gifted and Talented program for Indian Education provides the classroom with an electronic video microscope. Students Patricia C'Hair and Franklin Martel show how the TV monitor can display microscopic views to large groups.

programs, which increase knowledge of Native cultures. Native Americans hope that widespread learning about traditional ways will promote the respect they deserve as the first citizens of this country. They also hope that their children will receive an education that is equal in quality to that of other children in the United States.

However, in spite of reforms since the 1970s, Native American education continues to lag far behind that of other American education systems. Native students rank among the lowest of all groups in terms of academic achievement and have the highest dropout rate of any group in the United States.

U.S. Indian Higher Education

Until recently, education beyond high school was seen as unnecessary for Native Americans by many U.S. policymakers, who felt Indians would benefit more from job training than academic pursuits. Bacone College in Oklahoma and Fort Lewis College in Colorado both had small Indian populations in the late 1800s and early 1900s. These colleges, however, were the exception. In 1935, less than 1 percent of the Indian population attended college.

Change was slow. In the 1950s a few colleges established special programs to train teachers who might work on or near a reservation. In 1963, the first college preparatory program for Native Americans was established at Haskell Institute, which became a junior college two years later. There were some small, localized efforts through the 1960s to include more Native Americans in **higher education** systems. However, it was not until 1972 that a major piece of legislation was passed. The Indian Education Act, followed by additional legislation, began a shift in federal policy toward college education for Native Americans. Throughout the late 1960s and the 1970s, the number of Indian students enrolled in college increased by 500 percent. In other words, the number of Native college students was five times greater by the end of the 1970s.

Today, more Indians than ever are attending college. In 1968, only 181 Indians graduated from college. By 1988 and 1989, a total of 5,125 Indians graduated from

Indian student drum at annual University of California, Los Angeles, American Indian Student Association powwow.

college: 3,954 bachelor's degrees, 1,086 master's degrees, and 85 doctorates were earned.

Tribal Colleges

In 1966, the Navajo tribe created the first college in the United States controlled by a Native tribe. As a result of the success of the Navajo Community College, Congress passed legislation in 1978 providing support for additional tribal colleges. There are now 22 tribally controlled colleges in the United States. Tribal colleges vary greatly; some exist in trailers or abandoned buildings, while others enjoy large campuses comparable to many other community colleges.

Tribal colleges have made special efforts to help students achieve success. Because there is such a long history of academic failure on reservations, many students do not believe that they can succeed, or that college will be worthwhile. Some students carry generations of hostility toward schools.

Tribal colleges often begin by preparing Indian students to think of themselves as capable learners. Many Native students are older than the usual college age, or are single parents returning to school after a long absence. Learning skills, personal speaking, social skills, and other classes develop self-confidence in these and other Native stu-

Thebacha College Trades Complex, Fort Smith, Arkansas.

dents. Tribal colleges offer a wide range of courses. Many of these are designed to meet special needs of Native students.

The colleges also provide academic programs that prepare students to transfer to four-year colleges or universities. All tribal colleges include courses in Native languages and cultures, and most offer degrees in Native American Studies.

Tribal colleges also work with tribal elders and cultural leaders to write down and record traditional literatures and arts. Preserving cultural traditions is an important goal. Another goal is to extend these traditions out into the non-Indian communi-ty by sponsoring traditional activities and tournaments.

Clearly, tribal colleges have been successful. One survey found that students who attended a tribal college right after high school were eight times more likely to finish college than students who went to an off-reservation college.

Native American Studies Programs

Along with members of other minority groups in the 1960s and 1970s, Native Americans began to demand more control over their educational programs. One result was the establishment of several Native American Studies (NAS) programs at colleges and universities in the United States. The Red Power movement saw widespread Native American college education as a stepping-stone to national power and a stronger voice for the needs of Native Americans.

Native American Studies programs focus on preserving the culture and history of Native peoples and promoting an "Indian perspective" in many colleges and universities. Although most of the NAS programs are small, several offer a bachelor's or master's degree. Although NAS began in the United States, Native Studies programs can now be found in Canada, most of the American republics, and several European countries. Centers for Native people in New Zealand, Australia, and Norway have also been created.

Education among the First Nations in Canada

Before Europeans intervened, traditional Native education in present-day Canada was carried out through **informal education** and the experiences of daily life, as it was in the United States. Children were taught the ways of the tribe and family. Sacred teachings, instruction in hunting and fishing, and learning the roles of men and women were some of the "subjects" of Native children's education. Children learned tribal history and values through myths and legends, songs, ceremonies, and festivals. Education was an experience in which children learned to assume adult roles as members of the tribe, and to take their place in the community.

When they arrived on the North American continent, European settlers almost immediately set out to change all this. The goal of the French and British was to "civilize" the Indians and teach them European ways of life. They regarded the Indians as a primitive people with no religion or culture. They were determined to convert them to Christianity and turn them into "productive" citizens.

The French Attempt to Educate the Indians

The first permanent French settlement in Canada was established in Quebec in 1608. The French attempted to educate the Indians in their ways using a number of different methods. All ended in failure. Priests traveled to Indian villages, learned their languages, and attempted to convert them to Christianity. This failed because the Indians felt they already had a satisfying religion and way of life. They simply ignored the priests, and carried out their daily lives.

The French also began sending children with "potential" to France to be educated. The French thought that when they returned, these Natives would serve as role models for other Indians. This was a disaster. The change in lifestyle was too drastic for the young Indians. They could not cope with life in France, and they no longer fit into their own Indian society when they returned.

Another method of encouraging Native children to adopt European beliefs was to send Indian youth to Roman Catholic seminaries and boarding schools. Indian children found the studies irrelevant, and they longed for their families and homes. Most ran away, and the parents refused to send them back.

Another French attempt at re-educating Native peoples involved setting up reserves, or tracts of land near towns where Indians would live permanently. The reserves were considered a total educational experience. Each reserve would have a school, church, and hospital—all administered by missionaries. The French expected that Native peoples would learn to adopt a French lifestyle. This did not occur. Children were not interested in school, and adults did not learn farming, trades, or the French language. Reserves simply isolated Indians and allowed them to continue their own traditional way of life.

Canada's Native peoples believed that their ways were well suited to the environment in which they lived. They viewed education as a natural part of growing up and learning to assume one's place in the community. In contrast, the French methods of education were very authoritarian. Children were told what to do, rather than learning by doing. There were many rules, and the harsh discipline was foreign to Indian children. Reading and writing French seemed of little value to people whose lives depended on hunting and trapping. It is not surprising that the French attempts at enforcing their education systems on Native peoples failed.

Indian Education under the British and Canadians

When the British assumed control of Canada in 1763, they developed a policy toward Indians that was similar to the French. They tried to "civilize" the Indians. Unlike the French, however, who never took Indian land through treaties, the British signed treaties with the Indians that promised free education, among other things, in exchange for their lands.

Under early British rule, the first schools for Indians were day schools on the reserves set up by missionaries. Eventually the British government realized that the Indians were not giving up their traditional ways, and so it adopted the American practice of educating Indians in boarding schools. In these schools, as in their American counterparts, attendance was required. Children were removed from their homes by force when necessary.

In general, British-run boarding schools were a negative experience for Indian students. For ten months each year they were forbidden to speak their native languages or see their families. Most attended from the age of six until sixteen. By the time they graduated, many could no longer speak their Indian language. Many felt confused about who they were, and where they would fit in. Throughout their education they had been told that the Indian ways were worthless.

One third grader in a Catholic boarding school wrote this for his school newspaper:

I will listen when Sister reads to us in school, so that I can tell my parents when I go home for the holidays. We should never go to the sun dances, and we should try to stop it if we can by telling our parents it is forbidden by God. We should try to give good example to the children who do not come to school yet. I will never go to a sun dance.

At the same time that their traditional lifestyle was being devalued, very few Indians were able to gain enough skills from this educational system to comfortably support themselves in Canadian society. Even those who did were faced with discrimination and prejudice, which prevented them from getting jobs.

By the year 1900, Indians were no longer a priority for the Canadian government. Isolated on reserves, Native peoples often became economically dependent on the government. The government reacted to this by cutting back on money for the schools. The new policy was to give Indians minimal skills and let them return to the reserve. In 1930, only 3 percent of Indian children went past sixth grade.

The Reverend Ahenakew, a Cree who graduated from the University of Saskatchewan, urged the government in 1923 to change its policies toward Indians:

For those who ... survive [school] and graduate, during every day of their training they have acted under orders. They never needed to use their own minds and wills ... when suddenly given their freedom they do not know how to use it. Their initiative is lost.... [They] sit on the fence between the whites and the Indians, belonging to neither, fitting into neither world.... You cannot make a white man out of an Indian. It is much better to make us good Indians, for we are Indian in our person and our thinking.

Little changed, however. By 1950 only about 33 percent of Indian students went past third grade. In contrast, twice as many non-Indian Canadian children continued in school.

By 1950, the Canadian government admitted that its efforts to educate Indian children had been a failure. (The French had reached this same conclusion three hundred years earlier.) The British changed to a policy of integrating, or including, Indian children in the

EDUCATION IN THE NISGA COMMUNITY: AN EXAMPLE OF THE MOVEMENT TOWARD SELF-GOVERNMENT IN EDUCATION

In 1973 the Nisga Indians of Northern British Columbia spoke out about their children's need for an appropriate kind of high school education. The Nisga wanted bicultural (taking two different cultures into account), bilingual (using two languages) education and they wanted to participate in their children's education rather than sending them off the reserve to school. In 1974 British Columbia school officials agreed to create a separate Indian school district controlled by the Nisga. The Nisga community now elects the school board and handles all administration in their district. In 1975 most of the grade 7-12 students beginning at the new Nisga school were three to four years behind in reading, English, math, and science and had a 90 percent high school dropout rate. Four years later, students were only about one year behind the national average and the dropout rate had gone down dramatically, to about 20 percent.

Insarvik School, Repulse Bay (Inuit), 1992.

public school system. By 1960, about 25 percent of young Indians were attending public schools. The residential schools were closed. By 1980, almost 60 percent of Indian youth were enrolled in public schools, and an additional 32 percent attended federal day schools. Still, problems remained. In the 1970s and 1980s, between 60 percent and 80 percent of Indian students dropped out of school. This is more than double the drop-out rate for non-Indians in Canada.

The educational system itself was a main cause of Indian students' lack of interest in school. Traditional Indian education involved silent observation and a "hands-on" approach, with very little verbal instruc-

tion. Children would perform the skill when they felt they had completely mastered it. They were never tested, or expected to perform for an instructor. Low self-esteem, lack of family encouragement, lack of teaching about Indian life, and negative messages about Indian culture and history all contribute to the high dropout rate.

Indian Self-Determination

For over three hundred years, the responsibility for Indian education in Canada was taken over by the dominant society—French, British, and finally, Canadian. In the 1960s, a major shift began. This shift was fueled by the government's recognition of its failures, as well as increased activism among Indians and the general movement toward self-determination.

In 1972, the National Indian Brotherhood published a paper titled "Indian Control of Indian Education." This policy paper made it clear that parents and the local bands (tribes) must be in control of education. The policy said that Indian children must be given a strong sense of identity and confidence in their own personal worth. The government accepted this policy in 1973.

Since that time, much has happened. By the mid-1980s, 450 of Canada's 577 Indian bands were in control of all or part of the education for their children. In the public schools Indian culture is studied in several grades. The study of Indian culture is aimed at recognizing the contribution of Canada's First Nations and developing an appreciation for their ways. Training programs aim to develop more Indian teachers.

Native studies programs, as well as special Indian programs, are now offered in colleges and universities across Canada. In the mid-1970s, an Indian-controlled college, the Saskatchewan Indian Federated College, was founded.

Indian cultural survival schools have been established, which devote about half their time to teaching Indian culture. Indian materials are used for the academic subjects when possible. Science courses often stress ecology and the traditional Indian relationship between people and the environment. Many Indian teachers have begun to use books about Indian life that are written by Indians. One example is the *Mishomis Book: The Voice of the Ojibway*, by Edward Benton-Banai.

NEW CURRICULA

One of the most exciting developments in Indian education has been the growth of curricula from an "insider's" or Indian perspective. Many Indian educators have begun to produce curriculum materials for use in both Indian and public schools. A good example is *The Mishomis Book: The Voice of the Ojibway,* by Edward Benton-Banai, an Ojibway from Minnesota. The book takes the perspective of a *Mishomis* (grandfather) and *Nokomis* (grandmother) to tell Ojibway oral history and teachings. The book, written at the intermediate and senior levels, uses a storytelling mode to describe such topics as the Ojibway creation story; the origins and meaning of sacred ceremonies like the *Midewiwin,* pipe, and sweat lodge; the nature of the clan system; and legends and history. Ojibway words are used throughout. Increasingly, curriculum materials written from an Indian perspective are being used in classrooms in all grades to portray an accurate and sensitive picture of Indian people and their way of life.

Several schools feature a cultural survival camp, where staff and students go to a reserve for one week to live with elders in the traditional way. Elders teach students the traditional skills, tell stories and legends, and perform rituals such as sweat lodge and pipe ceremonies. Students also learn traditional values such as sharing, cooperation, self-reliance, respect, and responsibility by participating in the day-to-day running of the camp.

Some cultural survival schools hold a sweetgrass ceremony. In this ritual, braided sweetgrass is burnt and participants "smudge" themselves with the smoke. Each morning before classes, prayers are said, announcements are made, and issues are discussed in a traditional Indian talking circle.

Indian language immersion schools teach entirely in an Indian language in the early grades. English is introduced later. It is hoped that Indian languages will be preserved in this way. In addition, students will develop higher self-esteem and a stronger sense of themselves as Indians.

In 1975 there were only 53 Indian-controlled schools, and only 4 percent of Indian children attended them. By 1989, there were 300 Indian-run schools, enrolling nearly 40 percent of Indian children. The number of dropouts has steadily decreased. In 1960, only 3 percent of students were in their last year of high school; by 1989 this figure had jumped to 42 percent. Similar progress has been made in enrolling Indian students in colleges and universities. In 1960, there were only 60 students enrolled in college; by 1989, there were 18,535!

19
Native American Health

What Is Health?

Health is defined differently by different cultures. In most modern Western societies, health is seen as the absence of illness. In contrast, most traditional Indian societies view health as wellness, rather than the absence of sickness. Healers are often called upon to prevent illness or misfortune, to provide protection, or to bless happy occasions such as weddings or the birth of a child. They may offer thanks for a bountiful harvest or a successful hunt. In many Native American tribal groups health and religion are so closely related that healing is one of the main responsibilities of the religion. Many of the annual ceremonies are organized to help ensure the health and safety of the community.

Modern societies believe that diseases are caused by viruses or bacteria, or by lifestyle choices (such as smoking or diet). In contrast, Native societies believe that

Little Big Mouth, a medicine man, seated in front of his lodge near Fort Sill, Oklahoma, with medicine bag visible from behind the tent, 1869-70.

when man is in **harmony** with nature and the gods or great spirit, he is well. It is only when people are not in harmony that they become ill. A statement by Chief Sealth (also known as Chief Seattle) in 1854 summarizes this basic belief:

> The deer, the horse, the great eagle, these are our brothers. The earth is our mother. All things are connected like the blood which unites one family. Whatever befalls the earth, befalls the sons of the earth. Man does not weave the web of life. He is merely a strand in it. Whatever he does to the web, he does to himself.

Healers and Healing

Often American Indians and Alaska Natives will try various home remedies before calling for a healer. Sometimes these home remedies include a prayer to call for the help of a guardian spirit or ancestral **totem.** (A totem is a helping spirit that may be represented as a special animal or bird.) If these practices do not bring relief, then a healer is called.

Most tribes have different names for their traditional healers, but non-Indians have described these healers with words such as medicine man, medicine woman, **shaman,** Native practitioner, and traditional healer.

Usually healers work with patients in the patient's home. Depending on the tribe and the type of illness, the healing ceremony may require a few minutes, or may take as long as several days. In some cases, a series of different ceremonies may be held over a period of one or two years. The ceremony may involve singers, dancers, drummers, persons to prepare ceremonial objects, and elders who help prepare the dancers.

Tribal members may become healers in a variety of ways. They may serve as an apprentice to an experienced healer. Some may become healers by gaining membership in a healing society, often by being born into one. In some tribes, one may become a healer as a result of a special dream experience or vision. In such a vision, the healer may be given a special source of healing power, as well as a special song or special practices.

The training period for healers may take from 2 to 20 years. Among the Ojibway, it often takes over 21 years for a healer to become a full member in the Midewiwin, or Grand Medicine Society. Only the most

MEDICINE. LODGE.

Medicine Lodge. A patient lies in a Plains teepee. The Indian at left shakes a gourd rattle. The central figure, apparently the medicine man, holds a pipe in his right hand and the patient's wrist in the other. A drummer sits at right.

WORDS TO KNOW

epidemic: the rapid spread of a disease so that many people in an area have it at the same time.

harmony: a condition where feelings, ideas, and actions all work together smoothly; the idea comes from music, when several notes played at the same time seem to fit together to make up one sound that is pleasing.

holistic: concerned with all the aspects of health, including the physical, mental, emotional, and spiritual. *Holistic* medicine deals with the whole person—body, mind, and spirit.

immunity: resistance to disease; the ability to be exposed to disease without necessarily getting it.

shaman: a Native spiritual leader who is expected to heal the sick, see into the future, and help with activities such as hunting. *Shamans* usually have knowledge of the supernatural.

totem: an animal, bird, fish, plant, or other natural object that a person or group takes as its emblem or protective spirit.

senior and experienced healers may belong to this group. In addition to studying and training, candidates for the Midewiwin Society are expected to lead a blameless life and show such values as honesty, bravery, and humility.

In many tribes a healer is required to devote full-time work to studying and participating in healing ceremonies. In some, such as the Inuit, only men may be healers and only women can be herbalists (one who practices healing by the use of herbs) or midwives (one who assists in delivering babies).

In other tribes, the women may be the healers while the men participate in some other way, perhaps as dancers or drummers. For example, among the Pomo Indians of Northern California the healers are often women, but the men have an important role in the more public ceremonies such as the Big Head Dance. Healers spend considerable time training and teaching others the various ceremonial dances and songs, and they may supervise the creation of ceremonial objects.

Almost always, healers are considered to be spiritual or religious leaders. It is also common for healers to serve as key advisors to the tribal chief. Among the Pueblo, for example, the religious leader selects or nominates the governor for the pueblo each year. Today healers are also asked to assist in decisions about cultural and public health issues. Some healers may work with mental health programs or with schools to ensure that the curriculum has the proper cultural content.

Most healers in Native American communities see their role as initiating the healing process rather than actually curing the sick person. Through prayers, songs, and other related activities they call upon the spirits to help heal the patient, or to empower the patient to heal himself.

The career of a healer in most tribes does not bring wealth. Healers usually charge small fees, or none at all. Members of the tribe may contribute food and other necessities for the healer so he or she can devote full time to healing. In some cases, healers assist patients only on a part-time basis and are employed in another occupation as well.

The Role of Traditional Healers Today

Today most Native American babies are born in hospitals, and people requiring surgery or other special services are cared for by physicians in hospitals. Nevertheless, traditional healers are also used. They serve patients who have mental health problems, or a health problem that modern medicine has been unable to cure. Recurring bad dreams are an example of a reason to call a healer. Traditional healers are used more often today by tribal members who have not fully adopted the mainstream culture.

Traditional healers may coordinate a variety of ceremonies and other religious activities for the tribe. Depending on the tribe, healers may treat a number of patients at one time. For example, during a Sun Dance as many as a dozen people may be involved in a piercing ceremony.

Causes of Unwellness: Natural and Supernatural

Native American groups believe that illnesses are caused by either natural or supernatural forces. Natural causes are known causes, such as injury from falling off a horse, or stomach problems caused by something one ate. Many of these illnesses are mild and easily treated at home or by modern medicine. In cases where the problem is more severe, traditional healers may be called in to determine why it occurred and to prevent future mishaps.

Sometimes conditions are believed to be caused by failing to follow cultural rules or taboos. For example, a tribe may have a rule forbidding clan members to marry each other. If the child of such a marriage is born with a cleft lip, they may believe that this is punishment for the parents' failure to follow the rules. Ceremonies that include confession and setting things straight are often called for.

Most Indian tribes view humans, nature, and the supernatural (or spirits) as being on an equal footing. When this balance or harmony is disturbed, the individual or group is vulnerable to illness or misfortune. They may become ill or die as a result of an angry god. For example, a series of unexplained disasters such as a severe drought or **epi-**

Grey Squirrel, a medicine man, giving herbs to Rainbow Stevens, a patient, seated on a sand painting, 1963.

demic disease may be seen as punishment for failing to observe certain customs or ceremonies. Or a spirit may be engaged by another tribe member to harm an opponent. Some Native cultures believe that spells and witchcraft cause illness or misfortune. Objects such as pieces of a victim's hair or clothing may be taken and a spell woven to bring harm to an individual. The cure in this case is to retrieve the object, thus breaking the spell.

Plant and Animal Spirits

Nature, plants, animals, birds, and sacred places have great importance in tribal life. Certain animals such as eagles, bears, deer, or buffalo may be seen as powerful allies, whose spirits help to protect the group.

Plants and animals are central to many sacred ceremonies. Important food sources, such as salmon, buffalo, rice, and corn, are honored for their contribution to humans. For example, tribes who honor the buffalo often imitate the animals in their dances and call upon the animal spirits during times of illness or misfortune.

Plant spirits are also important in healing. Some tribes use Indian tobacco to help diagnose illnesses. Before contact with Europeans, tobacco was only used in healing ceremonies or as a gesture of good will when visitors came to discuss important topics. Tobacco is still used today in many healing ceremonies and offerings to the spirits. In addition to tobacco, other plants such as sage, cedar, and sweetgrass are used in healing rituals, or in herbal teas and medicines. Because plants are viewed as living beings, special songs and prayers are used to enhance their healing powers.

Modern and Traditional Ways

European medicines were introduced to most Indian tribes during the 1700s. Traders, missionaries, and army doctors sometimes cared for the sick. Some tribes included medical supplies or a doctor's services as part of their treaties with the government. In other words, they gave up some or all of their land in order to receive health care. In part, this was necessary because epidemics had wiped out so many tribes and reduced so many others to fragments that they lost their healers and were forced to rely on European medicine. Even today, a number of tribes do not have healers and must depend on healers from other tribes.

A major difference between Indian and modern medicine is that traditional healers

Medicine man helping a patient. Notice the bowl and pestle for mixing medicines. The medicine man is shaking a gourd rattle and may be singing a medicine song.

have always had a **holistic** approach. In other words, they treat the whole person—body, mind, emotions, and spirit. They also treat the person within his or her family or community, and take these into account as factors in the patient's well being. For example, in some Indian communities the healers may see alcoholism as being caused by failure to follow traditions and customs, as a result of European contact. Accepting European medicine was difficult for many tribal members, who found it strange that disease could be caused by germs or viruses that they could not see.

Traditional Indian healers developed very effective ways of dealing with illnesses. In the 1970s a historian found at least 170 mod-

DIFFERENCES IN CONCEPTS OF HEALTH

	Indian Medicine	Modern Medicine
Oriented to:	wellness	illness
Patient is treated:	with family or community	alone
Focuses on:	"why" illness occurred	"how"
Causes:	natural and supernatural	natural
Number of causes:	multiple	single

ern drugs that were previously discovered and used by Indian tribes in pre-European times. Some of these are digitalis, quinine, belladonna, cocaine (from coca leaves), curare, and ipecac. To find cures for cancer, AIDS, and other diseases, researchers have returned to the jungles of South America and other non-Western communities to question Native healers about plants and herbs and to conduct their own research.

In the 1950s, modern medicine became more available and more widely accepted among Native groups, but until that time traditional healers used a variety of treatments to cure illnesses. Herbal antiseptics were used even before Europeans adopted this as standard practice. Cautery (localized burning) to speed up healing or relieve pain was performed, usually with certain reeds or woods. Heat treatments, especially with herbs, were common. Fever treatment often called for rest, use of a sweat lodge, a special liquid diet, and anti-fever herbal medicine. Mineral springs were used for arthritis, muscle aches, and other purposes. Massages with herbs and ointments were common.

For broken bones, wet rawhide was applied to splints so that when they dried, the bone would be unmovable. Crutches,

stretchers, and arm slings were also used by various tribes. Special diets are frequently used as a form of treatment. Soft foods or a special liquid diet might be prescribed for abdominal pain or diarrhea. Diet was also used to cleanse the body of substances that were toxic or caused illness. A woman might be put on a special diet to restore her strength after delivering a baby. Certain foods were considered therapeutic and were used to restore a sick person's physical strength.

Until they were placed on reservations, most tribes practiced isolation techniques with certain illnesses. Sometimes the clothing, bedding, and belongings of a sick or deceased person were burned, and the entire camp area was abandoned. Changes in climate were prescribed for some illnesses. Most tribes decided where to locate summer and winter camps not only according to how much food could be found there, but also based on the sacredness of a place for healing ceremonies. Treatment of certain mental disorders, such as depression, often called for moving back to a familiar homeland.

The use of herbs continues to be an important part of healing practices of many Native Americans today. However, herbs are valued primarily for their essence or

Henry Crow Dog praying in a sweat lodge, 1969.

healing spirit, rather than for their biological properties alone. Songs and prayers may be said before the plants are harvested, and some plants may only be harvested or prepared by herbalists. Most Indian families keep their own supplies of home remedies for minor illnesses.

Native peoples learned to use plants for healing by observing nature and experimenting. They saw the effects of certain plants on the body, and they could predict outcomes. For example, in 1535 the Huron Indians cured French explorer Jacques Cartier's men of scurvy (a sometime fatal condition of bleeding and swollen gums caused by a lack of vitamin C). The Huron cured the scurvy with a tonic made from spruce buds. Spruce buds contain vitamin C, a discovery that would be recognized later by the Europeans.

Peyote

Peyote, a substance obtained from the button-like parts of the mescal cactus, is used as a sacrament and healing plant in the Native American Church. The plant heals, but is also used to create visions which teach the person the causes of his or her illness or misfortune. The peyote ceremony, which usually lasts one night, is used for a broad range of illnesses. It is also used for blessings and the ritual of thanksgiving. Peyote meetings may be requested by the family of one who will undergo major surgery in hopes of ensuring a successful outcome.

The American Indian Religious Freedom Act of 1978 formally allowed Native Americans the freedom to practice their religion. (The law also gave tribes the right to sacred lands and the right to possess sacred objects, such as eagle feathers.) Although this law is in effect, there are still many difficulties in actually practicing these freedoms. The use of peyote in religious ceremonies is legal in only nine states; other states consider it a controlled substance and bar its use.

European Contact and Native American Health

Doctors, traders, and explorers who made early contact with Native North Americans noted the exceptional good health of the people. They were clean, good-looking, without apparent illness, and peaceful. In a letter to the queen of Spain, Christopher Columbus called the Indians a race of hardy people.

This would soon change. The invading Europeans brought epidemic diseases that killed millions of Indians and wiped out whole tribes. Indians had no knowledge of illnesses such as smallpox, measles, tuberculosis, or typhoid, which were widespread in Europe. Europeans had built up some **immunity** (resistance) to these diseases, but the Native Americans had none. Therefore they were more likely to get the diseases when coming into contact with Europeans— and much more likely to die from them.

In one pueblo of New Mexico, five thousand Natives died of smallpox in 1780 and 1781. Many East Coast tribes lost over 90 percent of their members to this disease. For Indians, smallpox was a death sentence. In fact, Europeans actually used diseases such as smallpox as weapons against the Indians in an early form of germ warfare. Written records at Indian trading posts tell of soldiers giving blankets infected with smallpox to Indian communities. Men, women, and children alike died in mass numbers. The tribes could hardly defend themselves when deathly ill.

Once Indians were placed on reservations, close living quarters, poor nutrition, contaminated water, poor housing, and harsh weather conditions all contributed to the spread of diseases.

By 1890, the Native population of North America had dropped from more than two million to 250,000. Because of epidemic disease, starvation, warfare, and hardship, Native peoples were reduced almost to extinction.

Several things saved the American Natives from extinction. First, there was some help from the outside. Missionaries alerted non-Indians to the terrible living

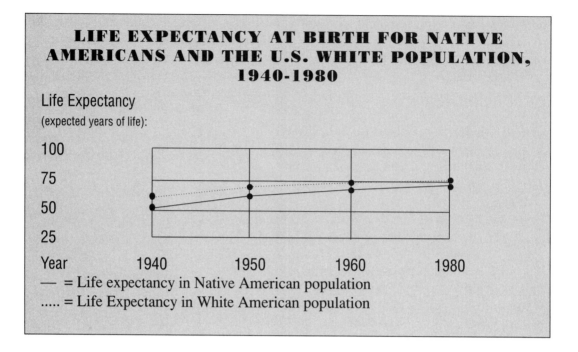

LIFE EXPECTANCY AT BIRTH FOR NATIVE AMERICANS AND THE U.S. WHITE POPULATION, 1940-1980

Life Expectancy
(expected years of life):

— = Life expectancy in Native American population
..... = Life Expectancy in White American population

conditions and loss of life of Native peoples. In 1849, the federal government created the Office of Indian Affairs, removing control of Native peoples from the War Department. Attention was given to living conditions on the reservations. Doctors and nurses began to provide health care services. These and later changes supported an increase in the Native population to almost two million by the year 1990.

Changing Lifestyles

Before Europeans came, most Native peoples lived a very healthy lifestyle. They lived off the land, taking up farming, hunting, and gathering. Physical exercise was a way of life. Conditions such as heart disease, diabetes, high blood pressure, alcoholism, and obesity were unknown. Today, living off the land is nearly impossible. The buffalo are gone, salmon fishing has been restricted,

cities have been built. Many of the health problems Native Americans face today are a direct result of the change in lifestyle that has been forced upon them.

The need for traditional healers has increased in recent years as more Indian communities take responsibility for their own health programs. Many of the "new" health problems faced by Native peoples are also new to Native healers, but the healers are able to use their skills to help patients cope with these diseases, or to accept modern medical treatment.

Today more Native health problems are a result of unhealthy lifestyles than poor medical care. Many tribes are searching for ways to prevent these problems by educating the young. They are encouraged to improve their nutrition, exercise, and view themselves more positively. Increasing

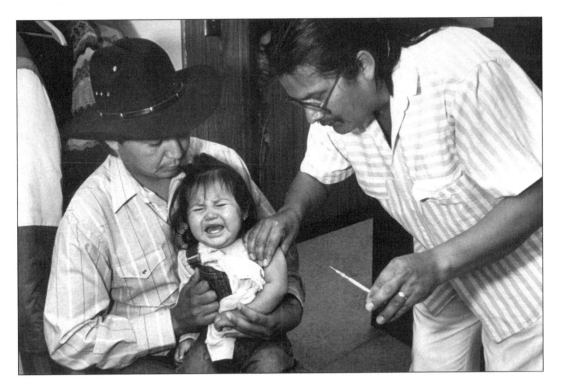

Albert Begay holds his daughter, 15-month-old Devona, after she was given a measles injection by nurse Ron Garnanez at the Shiprock Indian Hospital in New Mexico.

numbers of Native Americans are becoming doctors and returning to work with tribal groups. This leads to more blending of traditional and modern ways in health care and a greater appreciation for the role of culture in healing.

The Indian Health Service

Military doctors with the Department of War first offered health care to Indians in the 1800s. The first federal hospital for Indians was built in Oklahoma, also in the 1800s. Later in that century, the Office of Indian Affairs took over responsibility for Indian health from the War Department. Indian health care changed hands again in the 1950s, with the creation of the Indian Health Service (IHS). The IHS is a division of the U.S. Public Health Service in the Department of Health, Education, and Welfare.

As of 1990, the Indian Health Service operated 43 hospitals, 66 health centers, 4 school health centers, and 51 health stations. Native American tribes operate another 7 hospitals, 89 health centers, 3 school health centers, 64 health stations, 173 Alaska village clinics, and 6 community service centers. Since 1955 the number of health care workers has increased greatly. There are now over 9,000 health professionals working in the IHS, including over 770 doctors, 250

Entrance to medical buildings at Crow Agency, Montana.

dentists, and 2,000 registered nurses. The Indian Health Service is responsible for the health care of about 1.16 million Indians in the United States, primarily those living on reservations.

Several laws and acts of Congress expanded the role of government in Indian health care, beginning with the Snyder Act in 1921. The need for health care services for the growing number of Indians living in cities and large urban areas was not addressed until recently. The Indian Health Care Improvement Act (1976) and the Indian Health Care Amendment (1980) created funding for the health care of Indians living in cities and off the reservations in rural areas. These programs offer a number of services, but the health needs of off-reservation Indians are still largely unmet.

Because the Indian Health Service does not have funds to cover all Native health needs, they have set up a system of priorities.

The first priority is for life-threatening conditions. The second is a threatened loss of limb. Third priority covers conditions that can wait for up to 30 days. People who aren't ill enough to meet these criteria may have to wait until their condition worsens before they are eligible for treatment. Thus a mild, easily treated problem can develop into a serious, or even life-threatening condition that is very difficult and expensive to treat.

Contemporary Native Health in the United States

As of 1988, the five leading causes of death among Native Americans were: 1) heart disease, 2) accidents, 3) cancer, 4)

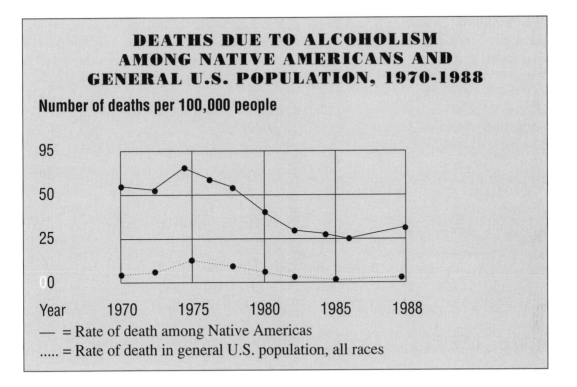

DEATHS DUE TO ALCOHOLISM AMONG NATIVE AMERICANS AND GENERAL U.S. POPULATION, 1970-1988

Number of deaths per 100,000 people

— = Rate of death among Native Americas

..... = Rate of death in general U.S. population, all races

cerebrovascular diseases, and 5) liver disease and cirrhosis.

Native Americans are four times more likely to die of alcoholism, four times more likely to die of tuberculosis, two and one-half times more likely to die of kidney failure, and over one and one-half times more likely to die of diabetes or accidents than the general U.S. population. Indian youth ages one to four are four times more likely to die from accidents than the national average. For the five- to fourteen-year-old age group, the rate of death from accidents is almost twice the national average.

From 1980 to 1982, the rate of death for Indians from liver disease and cirrhosis (a disease caused by excessive alcohol intake) was four times that of the general popula-

tion. It has been estimated that 75 percent of all accidental deaths among American Indians are related to alcohol. Alcoholism is considered the number one health problem facing American Natives today. Alcoholism contributes to many other forms of death and illness, including accidents, suicide, homicide, diabetes, birth defects, and pneumonia. Alcohol abuse has been related to half of all the crimes committed by adults on Indian reservations.

Contemporary Native Health in Canada

In Canada, the five leading causes of death for Native peoples in 1981 were: 1) diseases of the circulatory system, including heart disease; 2) accidents, including poisonings; 3) cancer; 4) respiratory disease, including pneumonia and tuberculosis; and 5) diseases of the digestive system, including liver disease and cirrhosis. The death rate for Native peoples from these five causes combined is one and one-half times greater than for non-Native Canadians.

Indians are from five to seven times more likely to die from infectious and parasitic diseases than the general population of Canada. From 1982 to 1985, the rate of death for the Indian population was four times higher than for the rest of Canada's people. The suicide rate is two to three times higher. The rate of infant mortality (infant deaths before the age of one year) is twice as high as for the general population.

Violence related to the use of alcohol and drugs has become widespread in aboriginal Canadian Indian communities. In 1978, from 30 to 60 percent of all accidental or violent deaths involved alcohol or drug abuse. A 1984 report estimated that 35 to 40 percent of adults and 10 to 15 percent of adolescents abuse alcohol. On northern and isolated reserves, it is believed that 25 percent of the children from ages 5 to 15 are gasoline inhalation abusers.

Physical injuries are the greatest cause of death among Natives aged 15 to 30. In some areas, the rate of death from injury in this age group is ten times the national average. The suicide rate for Indians under the age of 25 is six times higher than for non-Indians in the same age group. One-third of all deaths among Indian teenagers are suicides. Even more shocking is the belief that the suicide rate is actually much higher—many suicides may be reported simply as accidental deaths. The true rate of suicide among Indians may be as high as 12 times the national average. Some researchers believe that Canadian Indians have the highest suicide rate of any racial group in the world.

History and Causes of Canadian Native Health Problems

Early explorers and settlers often commented on the health and fitness of the Indian peoples living in the area of present-day Canada before the European conquest. Nicolas Denys wrote in 1672:

They were not subject to disease and knew nothing of fevers. If any accident happened to them ... they did not need a physician. They had knowledge of herbs, of which they made use.... They were not subject to the gout, gravel, fevers or rheumatism. The general remedy was to make themselves sweat, something which they did every month and even oftener.

Native healers had developed a very sophisticated and effective practice which involved several kinds of treatment. Herbs were used for pain relief, stomach and digestive problems, and many other disorders. Healers knew how to treat bone fractures and immobilize them. They used mouth-to-mouth resuscitation, which they called "putting the spirit back."

Native healers were experts in psychosomatic medicine (treating the mind and body at the same time to promote healing). One of their main techniques was the use of the sweat lodge. Sweatbaths are created by pouring water on hot rocks in order to purge the body, and ceremonies are conducted by a healer to clear the mind and spirit. Contemporary doctors think that some of the Indian healing ceremonies are so successful because they treat the mind and spirit, as well as the body.

In spite of their skills, Native healers were powerless against the new diseases brought by the Europeans. Smallpox, bubonic plague, tuberculosis, malaria, influenza, and other diseases destroyed entire tribes. In addition, Indians had no immunity to European "childhood diseases" such as measles, mumps, and whooping cough. Before Columbus, there were about one million Indians the area of Canada. One hundred years later, 90 percent of these Native peoples were dead. By the 1900s, entire generations of Indian people were gone and those who remained were reduced to conditions of poverty and dependence on the government. The use of alcohol caused the people to become demoralized, and their societies disintegrated.

In 1979, Noel Starblanket expressed the Indian view of the root causes of their health problems:

To be forced to live a life that is totally out of one's control is a source of constant stress, and leads to the weakness and demoralization of individuals and entire communities. We as Indian peoples have been forced into ... dependence. [This] has contributed to ... alcohol and drug abuse, family breakdown, suicides, accidents, and violent deaths. There is increasing scientific evidence that the stress of dependence and uncertainty leads to physical sickness as well.

The living conditions for most Canadian Natives are far below the standards enjoyed by the rest of the Canadian population. In 1980, the average income of Canadian Indians was only $3,300.

This was about one-third of the national average. Only 38 percent of Indians are employed, compared to 63 percent of the general population. In 1984, it was found that 47 percent of reserve housing was inadequate; 38 percent lacked one or more basic amenities, including running water, indoor toilets, baths, or showers. There is a lack of clean water, and waste disposal systems are inadequate on many reserves. In 1986, 45 percent of Indians had no high school education.

Canadian Health Systems

In the early 1900s, traditional healing was forcefully discouraged by the government, along with Native languages and cultures. This was part of the government's goal of forcing assimilation on Indian peoples into Canadian society (making them "blend in"). It was not until the 1970s and 1980s that the value of traditional healing was recognized, and a more tolerant attitude came about.

In 1905, Dr. P.H. Bryce was appointed by the Canadian federal government to combat tuberculosis, which was widespread among Indian communities. In the years that followed, responsibility for Indian health shifted to various departments. In 1962, the Medical Services Branch (MSB) was created within the Department of Health and Welfare. The goal of the MSB is to help Indian and Inuit peoples to achieve the same level of health as other Canadians.

Community Involvement in Health Care

By the late 1970s, it had become obvious that the problems of Indian health could not be solved simply by treating diseases. Any real improvements would have to be made by treating the causes of Indian ill-health. Social breakdowns, poverty, environmental problems, and cultural issues would all have to be treated.

In 1978 the World Health Organization (WHO) defined health as a state of complete physical, mental, and social well-being—not just the absence of disease. (Interestingly, this holistic approach is almost identical to traditional Native beliefs about health.) WHO went on to recommend that communities and individuals participate in planning and operating health care programs. In 1979 the Canadian government adopted a new Indian health policy with two important features: 1) all the needs of Indian communities should be addressed, not just treatment of disease; and 2) health programs should be created and controlled by the Indian communities themselves.

The Health Program Transfer Initiative was designed to give control of health programs to Native peoples. The transfer program has gradually been adopted by Indian Nations during the 1980s. Native reaction to this transfer has been mixed. Some bands see it as a good opportunity to take control over health services. Others see it as a way for the government to avoid its responsibility for Indian health. Indian health care has always been considered a treaty right (guaranteed by treaties); some Indians fear that the transfer of health care control will cause them to lose rights and services.

New partnerships are being developed between government and Native peoples, with a goal of empowering Indians to take control of their own destiny. It remains to be seen how changes in health care for Canadian Indians will address the many pressing problems facing the First Nations.

20

Native Americans and the Environment

FACT FOCUS

- Native North Americans share the spiritual view that all things—animals, plants, the sun and moon, rain and thunder, and people—are part of the complex life system of the natural world, and that human beings are not superior to other parts. Native attitudes about the environment reflect this belief.
- Early Native Americans intentionally set fires to beneficially alter the environment, increasing game and grazing land, encouraging new plant growth, and restoring forests.
- Although Native American religious beliefs emphasize respect for nature, Indian cultures have always made effective use of the environment to provide for their needs.
- Reservation lands have proven to be rich in resources such as coal, timber, gas, oil, and uranium.

For many years, non-Indians have romanticized Indians' spiritual relationship with nature. When pollution from factories and cars seems to be destroying the air and water, and nuclear fallout, chemical wastes, and pesticides seem to be destroying the land, people tend to long for the simpler ways of life that they imagine Indians once led. Yet many non-Indians, not really understanding Native American environmentalism, believe that these ways of life are too primitive to be practical in modern America, where industry supplies our everyday needs.

Before Europeans arrived, the present-day United States was home to ten to twelve million American Indians living in thousands of tribal groups that managed the land in their own particular ways. Native Americans have always used nature to fulfill their needs. Although the traditions of most Indian groups stress respect for the environment, they do not prohibit making effective use of technology. Throughout history, American Indians have shown a remarkable ability to make effective use of natural resources, while maintaining cultural and spiritual beliefs that emphasize high regard for the earth.

Before the fur trade with Europeans began in North America, many Native groups were careful to conserve the animals that they hunted. **Conservation** techniques with resources such as salmon, buffalo, or deer not only protected the groups' livelihood, but was also a part of many Native religious practices.

One example of early Native American skill in resource management was the many uses Indian cultures made of fire to beneficially alter the environment. In the East and Southeast, burning changed forest lands into mixed grasslands and young trees. This created feeding grounds for deer, hare, beaver, turkey, and other game. In the prairie areas, fire created additional grazing lands for buffalo. In the Southwest, the Apache and Papago used fire to keep grasslands from turning into chaparral (a dense area of thorny shrubs or dwarf trees).

Many tribes used fire for hunting, because it would drive game in a particular direction. Also, the fire would encourage new plant growth, which increased the amount of game. In California and the Pacific Northwest, fires rid forests of debris and allowed more desirable trees to grow. Modern foresters today realize that setting small fires can decrease undergrowth. This decreases the chances of a major forest fire.

Native Americans managed their resources in other ways as well. Cultivation, irrigation, and pruning of wild plants (even by gatherers), were common. The Ojibway of the Great Lakes would replant portions of their fields after harvesting wild rice. Plants

---

WORDS TO KNOW

conservation: protection and preservation of something; a carefully planned management system to prevent exploitation, destruction, or overuse.

trust; trust relationship: property that is held by one party for the use and benefit of another. Indian reservation land is held in *trust* by the U.S. government, meaning that it cannot be taxed or sold by the government and that the government must act in the best interests of Indians.

---

were managed for use in baskets, clothing, and tools as well.

Spiritual Beliefs Regarding Nature

Although spiritual beliefs vary among North American tribes, they all share the view that the human and non-human world are one. Spiritual powers reside in animals, birds, fish, plants, the sun and moon, the rain and thunder, and people as well. Human beings are only one part of a complex natural world and are not superior to the other parts. Native Americans' use of natural resources reflects this attitude.

Prayers, rituals, and religious ceremonies are part of daily activities in many Indian cultures. Native peoples may pray to the spirits of the animals they hunt, the plants they gather, or the fish they catch. Prayers and rituals allow the use of the resource, while respecting the spiritual power in it.

Native American cultures had a more humble concept of the place of humans in

Coolidge Dam on San Carlos Apache Reservation, Arizona.

nature than did the European settlers. Indians viewed the natural world as beyond their control, although they did believe they could predict what might happen. These attitudes are in direct conflict with the values of industrial societies. In order for industries to develop, vast quantities of natural resources are used up. Industry and its by-products often pollute the environment.

The more industrialized a society becomes, the more distance is created between producer (one who makes a product) and consumer (one who buys or uses a product). For example, hunters and farmers kill or produce the food their families eat. Workers in industrial societies do neither. They spend their days producing goods that will be consumed by distant people they may not even know. They work at specialized tasks in large organizations. This means that industrial workers often have little control over the final product that their company makes.

In a system such as this, nature is easily seen as the material to be used to make a product, rather than as an important part, in itself, of the whole life system on the planet. In an industrial society, nature is viewed mainly in terms of its use for human life. In this realm people feel they have the right to consume, conquer, and pollute nature.

Conflicts over the use of the environment and resources occur often between Native

Wyoming Indian Elementary School students show the radio collars they decorated. The collars were put on antelope that were released on the Wind River Indian Reservation.

peoples and business interests. For example, a hydroelectric plant may require flooding large areas, which makes hunting and trapping in the area impossible. Quite often, Native Americans find themselves competing for their resources. This competition frequently focuses on environmental issues.

Reservations and the Environment

The establishment of reservations changed the relationship between Indians and their environment. Before reservations, Indians lived on their traditional homelands, using local resources to supply their needs for food, shelter, and clothing. After being removed to reservations, this was often no longer possible. Most reservation lands were not good for agriculture. Often the reservation was not in the original territory of the tribe, or tribes were forced to share lands with other tribes, some of whom were enemies. Traditional lifestyles and land use were disrupted.

On the other hand, the reservations were often rich in new types of resources, such as coal, timber, gas, oil, and minerals like uranium. Over 50 percent of all known reserves of uranium in the United States are found on reservations. Reservations also hold 30 percent of all low-sulfur coal reserves, and 25 percent of oil reserves.

The government did not intend to give

away resources to Native Americans. These resources were unknown when treaties were signed and Indians were relocated to reservations in the late 1800s. In fact, when the government discovered that the resources existed, the treaties were changed or eliminated. For example, 18 treaties were negotiated just before and during the Gold Rush of 1849 in California. These treaties were never ratified (approved) by the U.S. Senate for fear that the lands might contain gold.

Land Use and the Government

Before reservations were established, Indian tribes decided how to use the land and controlled their own territories, usually without interference. The U.S. government took away this control. Reservation lands were not given free and clear. They are held "in trust," which means that the government still owns the land, but allows the Indians to use it.

Because they are held in **trust,** the use of reservation lands is governed by very complicated regulations, as well as by tribal laws and customs. The government must act in the best interests of the tribe, but the tribe may not always agree with the government's definition of what is best. In the early 1900s, it was common for the government to make decisions about land use and sign leases without even telling the tribes.

One result of government control of Indian lands has been serious environmental problems. Earlier in the twentieth century the Bureau of Indian Affairs negotiated leases on Indian land without regard to the wishes of the tribe. People who held leases often left behind polluted water and land. Leaking pesticide containers and under-

ground storage tanks for gas have been common. Waste disposal systems on the reservations do not meet federal standards and are a major source of pollution and related health problems. The government has not dealt with these problems, and the tribes do not usually have the money to solve them.

Because of the complicated way reservations are governed by state and federal laws, many laws which restrict pollution do not apply to Indian lands. Another problem is that the federal government has the responsibility to enforce environmental laws on reservations, but no money was set aside for that purpose. Even though states received millions of dollars for environmental protection, no funds were given to tribes for similar purposes. Recently this has changed, but tribes still do not receive as much money as the states and their problems are as severe, if not more so.

Tribal Management of Natural Resources Today

Today many Indian tribes are taking the lead in managing their natural resources and protecting the environment. There are many examples. The Salish-Kootenai have set aside 89,500 acres of the Flathead Reservation in Montana as a wilderness area, especially to protect the grizzly bear habitat. The Confederated Tribes of both the Yakima and the Warm Springs Reservations have set aside reserves where hunting is forbidden. In Arizona, the Tohono O'Odham and the Pima-Maricopa at Gila River have strong native plant protection programs. The Klamath of Oregon have devoted significant tribal resources to a fishery management program. This program is designed to restore the fish species traditionally used for food from their current endangered status.

Canadian Native protesting before Parliament.

Environmental Issues in Canada

In the northern part of Canada aboriginal peoples still depend directly on the land and its resources for their support and engage in hunting, fishing, gathering, and trapping to a greater degree than people in the southern part of Canada. Because of their relationship to the land, northern aboriginal peoples often find themselves in conflict with the government and private industry over environmental issues, especially during the last 20 years.

One of the earliest battles was over a huge hydroelectric plant in northern Quebec. The project, begun in the early 1970s, drew strong protest from the Cree and Inuit people who lived in the vast areas the Quebec hydro company was prepared to flood. The Natives' opposition led to court battles, a citizens campaign, and, finally, to a claims agreement by which the Cree and Inuit received a significant amount of money for the lands they lost, as well as sole ownership of other lands and the right to share management of their original lands. They have used

Inuit man ice fishing.

Another major struggle was opposition by the Dene and Inuit to a large-diameter pipeline in the Mackenzie River Valley. The pipeline was intended to ship Alaskan oil and Canadian natural gas from the Arctic to southern markets. The Dene felt that this development would eventually destroy their ability to live from hunting, fishing, and trapping. They also saw that benefits from this pipeline would go to distant corporations with no interest in their territory. The Dene would not benefit at all from the development. In the end, the Mackenzie Valley conflict ended with cancellation of the project, although a smaller pipeline was built there later.

These struggles resulted in a new process of public hearings before developments would be approved. The resistance of Canada's First Nations also resulted in the government starting a negotiation process to settle land claims. There are still many conflicts over land and resource use, but newer environmental laws have attempted to accommodate the native peoples' knowledge and use of the land.

the money to develop their economy through a variety of enterprises.

21
Art

- Native Americans have been producing art for over 25,000 years.
- "Tourist Art" is art created especially to provide souvenirs for tourists.
- In Canada no totem poles were built between 1884 and 1969, because the Canadian government outlawed it.
- In some Native American societies, everyone was expected to create and decorate artistic objects. Among other groups, most of the art was done by certain people who were especially skilled or talented.
- Before the mid-1900s, most Native American art was unsigned and the name of the artist was unknown to people outside his or her tribe.
- Native North American songs vary according to tribe and geographic area. A knowledgeable listener can often tell what tribe or area a song came from by its style, form, rhythm, or the way the instruments are used.
- In a Plains powwow song, a lead singer starts with one musical phrase sung as high as possible. Chorus members repeat his phrase with variations, then all sing the melody together. This is repeated in a variety of patterns with the pitch becoming lower and lower each time.

What Is Native North American Art?

In western European-based societies art is often isolated in museums, framed and hung in private homes, or used to illustrate books. In many cases, art is simply looked at. When Europeans first saw Native North American art, they thought Indians had no art—only crafts. The Europeans assumed that all art should be similar to European art. They failed to recognize and appreciate the many forms of art created by Native peoples.

Actually, Native Americans have a long and rich history of producing art, extending back some 25,000 years or more. For Native Americans, art is an expression of themselves and their values that is created to please the spirits as well as the senses. Most Native American art, however, is not made just to be looked at, but is woven into the very fabric of life. Decorations on clothing, pottery, baskets, carvings on totems, drawings and etchings on stone, figures engraved on the shaft of a war club, blankets woven with symbolic meanings—all these are forms of Native American **visual arts**. Music, dance, ceremonies, rituals, and festivals are also art forms.

Native North American Art History

Native American art has existed as long as people have inhabited North America—perhaps about 25,000 years. Native American art history can be divided into three periods: prehistoric, colonial, and contemporary.

The prehistoric period began about 25,000 B.C. and ended when writing was introduced in any given area, usually by way of European explorers, missionaries, and settlers. Most tribes came into contact with Europeans sometime between 1500 and 1800 A.D., depending on where they lived. The colonial period therefore extends from the date of contact with Europeans (1500-1800 A.D.) to 1900. The contemporary period is from 1900 to the present.

Prehistoric Native North American Art (25,000 B.C. to A.D. 1500-1800)

Most prehistoric art has been discovered by archaeologists (people who unearth and study ancient cultures). But it has also been found by farmers plowing their fields, bulldozers at construction sites, or looters looking for valuable goods. Except for "rock art," the oldest artworks found in North America date back to about 3000 B.C. Most Native American art did not survive because it was made of wood, hide, or fibers which rarely last long in moist soils.

It is interesting to note that Native Americans purposely chose materials that would

---

WORDS TO KNOW

drums: groups of Indian men singers (and recently women singers, too) often from different tribes, who get together to perform at powwows or other gatherings.

image: a picture or representation of something; for example, a warrior might dream of an eagle and then draw an *image* of the eagle on his teepee.

pictograph: an ancient painting or drawing on a rock wall.

petroglyph: a carving on a rock wall.

symbol, symbolic meaning: a *symbol* is something that stands for or represents an idea, emotion, or any other concept; for example, to some cultures the eagle is a symbol of power and strength. A *symbolic meaning* is the idea that the symbol represents; for example, the symbolic meaning of the eagle is power and strength.

visual arts: art forms that aim to please solely through the eye, as opposed to dramatic arts or literature, which also involve reading or listening. Examples of *visual arts* are painting, photography, sculpture, textiles, and pottery.

---

not last. This is one of the ways in which American Indian art differs from Western art. For most Native peoples, the important thing about an artistic object was its usefulness and its spirit power. They were not at all interested in creating lasting memorials to their skill as artists.

Petroglyph, Galisteo, New Mexico.

Rock Art

Rock art includes **pictographs** (paintings) and **petroglyphs** (engravings). The tradition of painting and carving on rock surfaces was probably brought to North America with its earliest immigrants about 25,000 years ago.

There are hundreds of sites of rock art throughout the United States and Canada. The Canadian Shield, for example, which extends from Quebec to Saskatchewan, contains hundreds of pictographs, and a smaller number of petroglyphs. Petroglyph sites are more common in the Eastern Woodlands of the United States.

Some of the most outstanding petroglyphs in North America are found at Nanaimo on Vancouver Island, British Columbia, and at Writing-on-Stone Provincial Park in southern Alberta. At Writing-on-Stone there are scenes describing battles and other activities in great detail. **Images** of horses, carts, and rifles show that rock art continued to be created well after contact with Europeans.

The most vivid pictographs in Native North America are located in the territory of the Chumash people in southern California. In this mountainous area, brilliantly colored pictures of humans and animals, as well as

284

The humpback flute player Kokopelli, with horned serpent (Utah).

abstract and circular patterns, are painted on rocks and in caves. It is believed that these images served a religious purpose and were inspired by visions resulting from trance states (dream-like experiences).

Changes in Art after 1000 B.C.

Throughout North America, prehistoric art varies from one culture area to another. This art has also changed over time. For example, changes in the forms and meaning of art began to occur more rapidly about 1000 B.C. One of the main reasons for this change was the introduction of agriculture and the beginnings of settled village life in the American Southwest, Southeast, and Midwest, and in the Great Lakes area of both Canada and the United States.

In the Arctic, major developments in art occurred between 500 B.C. and A.D. 1000. In Alaska and the islands of the Bering Strait, what is now called the "Old Bering Sea" style of ivory carving developed during this period. The peoples living there produced exquisitely carved bone, ivory, and antler objects in the form of humans, animals, and birds. In the Canadian high Arctic between 800 B.C. and A.D. 1000, an early Inuit culture also carved bone, ivory, and antler. These objects often showed several images in one work and had religious meaning.

On the Northwest Coast, the prehistoric Marpole culture (500 B.C. to A.D. 500) is known for its remarkable stone and bone carvings, which included ceremonial bowls, human and animal figures, and various utensils.

In New York state and southern Ontario, the prehistoric Iroquoian (A.D. 900 to 1600) produced pottery decorated with realistic and geometric designs. Antler and bone combs and figures and stone and clay effigy pipes were produced in abundance. The effigy pipes were used in the ritual smoking of tobacco and were decorated either with human figures or with birds, lizards, turtles, snakes, or bears—whatever represented the spiritual guardian of the pipe's owner.

The Eastern Woodlands area in prehistoric times is noted for its large ceremonial centers with burial mounds and temple mounds, open plazas, and elaborate art works. The people of this area used materials such as copper and mica, as well as the more common stone, shell, and clay.

Of all the prehistoric art traditions in Native North America, however, those of the American Southwest are considered the most

Carving of Hopi kachina.

dred different kachina dolls. Kachina dolls were used for teaching young children.

Pueblo peoples also produced pottery which was painted with figures and geometric designs in red, black, and white. Pottery making continued through the historic and contemporary periods. Today Pueblo pottery is made mainly for sale to tourists and collectors.

Native Art in the Colonial Period

The colonial period dates from first contact with Europeans (anywhere from A.D. 1500 to 1800, depending on the region) to about 1900. Native art of this period is better known and understood than prehistoric art, because examples have been collected, sketched, or described by explorers, traders, missionaries, artists, and scholars for over three hundred years.

Many Native works of art are now in museums throughout the Western world. As a matter of fact, very few artworks from the colonial period remain within their Native communities. Recently, however, some Native American works of art have been returned to their original communities, because Native people wish to preserve their history and culture.

Contemporary Native North American Art

Contemporary art in Native North America varies widely in form, meaning, and use. Traditional arts are created by Native Americans both on and off the reservation. Some art is made for private use within a community, and some is made for the general public to see. Some art is made mainly, or only, for sale to non-Natives.

notable. The Anasazi tradition of the prehistoric Southwest is very significant because it leads directly into the living culture of modern Pueblo peoples. The Anasazi tradition began with the Basketmaker culture, dating between A.D. 1 and 700. The Basketmaker people built underground houses that survive in modern Pueblo cultures in the form of ceremonial underground kivas (religious centers). The Basketmaker people also produced baskets with geometric patterns.

Supernatural "kachina" spirits were believed to visit the Pueblo peoples from time to time. Anasazi artists represented the kachina spirits in leather masks and some four hun-

Watercolor of Southwestern Indian children by Earl Sisto for 1992 UCLA Indian Child Welfare Conference.

Some Visual Art Trends among Native North American Communities

There are many varieties and styles of Native American visual arts in the United States and Canada. Some artists focus on subjects and use methods that reflect their traditions. Others mix contemporary methods with traditional subject matter. Some represent contemporary Indian issues with traditional styles. Many Native American artists have been schooled in Western art institutions and may or may not focus on their heritage or its traditional uses of art.

Indian communities often develop artistic styles that develop into what is called a "school" of art—a group of people who are under the same artistic influences. Because art is not only a reflection of individual vision, but also of the artist's experience as part of a culture, similarities within communities are not surprising.

In the Canadian Northwest Coast, totem poles and masks, dancing blankets, and other ceremonial objects are once again a major art genre after a long period of being forbidden. Production of these objects was suspended when the Canadian government outlawed potlatch ceremonies in 1884. After the ban was lifted, production resumed. The first "new" totem pole was raised in the Haida village of Masset, British Columbia, in 1969. Northwest Coast artists also produce ceremonial items for sale to outsiders, as well as art works that are adapted to European and American tastes, such as jewelry and sculpture.

The art of the Inuit of the Canadian Arctic and Alaska has had great success in the marketplace. Inuit sculpture, prints, drawings, and wall hangings are all in demand. In the 1950s the Inuit learned the Western and Japanese techniques of drawing on paper and making prints. By the 1970s, Inuit prints (stonecuts, silkscreens, engravings, and etchings) had become very popular. By the 1980s, the Inuit were selling more prints than sculpture. Inuit art uses both traditional and modern subjects. Some Inuit depict life in the twentieth century, complete with airplanes, snowmobiles, and Christian **symbols**.

In the American Southwest, the Navajo, Hopi, San Ildefonso, and Zuni Pueblo peoples continue to produce handwoven fabrics,

Kwakiutl totem poles at Alert Bay, around 1910.

painted pottery, baskets, and silver jewelry. They are maintaining traditions that reach back over two thousand years. The Navajo still make handwoven blankets on their reservation using the traditional vertical loom. Most Navajo weaving is done by women, whose work preserves traditional geometric patterns and sometimes includes pictures.

The "Southwest Style" of painting emerged between 1910 and 1960. Southwest style paintings depict historic ceremonial dances, hunting scenes, and daily activities in a two-dimensional style, using pale colors.

On the Plains, a similar style of painting arose in the 1940s. Plains artists as far north as the Canadian prairies painted in what was sometimes called the "Oklahoma" style. These works revealed a longing for traditional culture with subjects like buffalo hunts and brilliantly costumed warriors doing ceremonial dances.

Contemporary Style and Method in Visual Arts

The Woodland School (or the Legend Painters) was a school of artists working in the 1970s. They chose traditional subjects and styles, but used non-traditional materials and techniques, such as acrylic paint on canvas. Ojibway painter Norval Morrisseau, the inspiration of the school, paints brilliantly colored and often very large canvases using synthetic acrylic paints. This style and method is typical of Euro-American painting techniques of the 1960s. Morrisseau's subject matter is taken from such differing sources as traditional Algonkian pictography, rock art, and the stained glass windows of his childhood Catholic church.

There are some well-known contemporary Native artists in the United States and Canada who are not trained in traditional Native techniques, but who studied in leading Western art schools. These artists consider themselves artists first and foremost, and they express personal feelings and beliefs through their art, whether or not the subject matter has to do with Native American issues. They find no reason to limit themselves to one set of issues. Like anyone else, their work is informed by their identity and background and, to greater or lesser extents, reflects the spiritual and cultural values of their Native traditions. One such artist, Ojibway Carl Beam, uses his art to express his concerns about loss of spiritual

Nora Naranjo-Morse, *Pearlene Teaching Her Cousins Poker,* 1987.

values, the destruction of the environment, the dehumanizing effects of technology, and human cruelty and violence. His works blend images taken from photographs and newspapers with painted images and three-dimensional objects, such as feathers and even stuffed birds.

In some communities artists are once again practicing art forms that had not been practiced in decades. For example, in the 1970s Haida artist Bill Reid erected a totem pole in his ancestral homeland in Canada. It was the first pole carved and raised in over 100 years. Since then many other Haida artists have revived carving, printmaking, and ceremonial traditions with renewed interest. The Haida want their children to learn and respect the arts that are part of their heritage.

Many artists play with the idea of mixing Native and non-Native cultures. An example is Nora Naranjo-Morse, from Santa Clara Pueblo in New Mexico. In *Pearlene Teaching Her Cousins Poker,* Nora Naranjo-Morse takes the Pueblo image of ritual clowns (indicated by their striped bodies), makes them female instead of male, and shows them playing a game of poker, which they are learning from a book. With her wit and sense of play, Naranjo-Morse displays her view of the merging of modern and traditional ways. By using clay, she honors her mother and grandmothers and other female ancestors who made fine pottery.

"Tourist" Art

Tourist art is created specifically to sell to tourists as souvenirs. Sometimes tourist art is called "souvenir art" or "airport art." Carvings made of black argillite (a shiny black stone) by the Haida of British Columbia, Pueblo pottery, Hopi and Zuni Kachina dolls, beadwork moccasins, and other items are produced in large quantities for sale to outsiders. Today the tourist art business is booming so much that sometimes "Native American" art is also produced by workers in Taiwan, Japan, and Korea.

Traditional Arts of Men and Women

Among Native American societies of the past, many activities were divided according to gender. In other words, men and women had well-defined roles as artists. This continues to be true today, but to a lesser extent. An illustration can be found among the peoples of the Plains and Eastern Woodlands. Here, men and women made and decorated different types of objects.

Sally Karatak at museum in traditional Inuit beaded dress, Yellowknife, Northwest Territory.

Native American Women's Art in the Plains and Woodlands

In general, Plains and Woodlands women worked with fiber, animal hides, and ceramics. They engaged in weaving, sewing, and modeling to produce and decorate clothing, baskets, pottery, and certain kinds of utensils.

In particular, a woman's ability to produce finely decorated clothing was a measure of her success as an individual. Among many Plains tribes, women quill and beadworkers belonged to professional artists' guilds (or associations). Designing beautiful clothing and other artistic work brought honor to women. George Bird Grinnell, who lived among the Cheyenne in the 1890s, observed that in the artists' guild meetings the women gathered to recall and describe the fine works they had done in the past, just as men gathered to "count coup," or tell stories of their bravery in battle. Even today, expert Crow beadworker Winona Plenty Hoops says that "a good design is like counting coup."

In the Southwest, Pueblo women made pottery to carry water, store grain, mix dough, and for other uses. Female elders taught young girls how to make pottery. Nearly all Pueblo pottery was decorated. The teachers simply told their students to

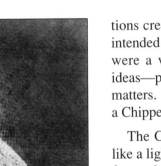

A turn-of-the-century artist paints traditional Haida patterns on a hat of woven spruce root.

"dream" their designs and offered no further instruction. The pottery designs that resulted were usually unique, yet similar to other patterns found in a particular tribe. A Zuni jar and its decorations are different from a Hopi jar, for example. Apparently Zuni girls dreamed of Zuni patterns, and Hopi girls dreamed of Hopi patterns.

Eastern Woodlands and Plains Men's Art

In the Eastern Woodlands and Plains, men used wood, bone, antler, and stone to produce bowls, spoons, weapons, pipes, and other objects. Often these would be decorated with images, such as a bird standing on the handle of a wooden ladle. The decora-

tions created on these objects were not just intended to make them look attractive. They were a visual language meant to express ideas—perhaps personal history or spiritual matters. An illustration is the decoration of a Chippewa war club.

The Chippewa war club itself is shaped like a lightning bolt, which represents power from the spirits in the sky. An eagle engraved on the side might represent an eagle that appeared to the warrior in a dream, a spiritual vision promising him protection and help. The owner would also engrave a series of horizontal stripes on the side of the club, each referring to a war expedition. Thus, the war club showed that war was a dangerous activity requiring the help and protection of the spirits. It also made a statement about the success that resulted from communicating with the spirit world.

During the 1800s, Plains Indians who were able to get pencils and paints recorded their war efforts in ledger books or notebooks. Today these drawings and paintings are known as "ledger book art." These artworks usually focus on a particular episode in which the warrior had been successful. Men also painted pictures of their spiritual experiences and visions. Plains shields were often painted with powerful spirit images, as were some teepees, articles of clothing, and hand drums.

On the Northwest Coast, the best-known carvings are the tall totem poles of the Haida and Tsimshian. Totem poles were built when a chief claimed the name of one of his deceased ancestors. Totem poles are carved from a length of a cedar log. A series of animal and human figures are stacked one on top the other; each represents an

Modern-day British Columbia artist Vicor Mowatt works traditional Haida patterns into a cedar box.

event in family history, particularly those with spiritual meaning.

Art and Environment

In each area of North America, Native American artists have created art that reflected the environment around them. For example, Northwest Coast peoples have used cedar wood for their arts for over one thousand years. Totem poles, masks, dance rattles, great storage boxes, and feasting bowls were made and used by these groups. Northwest Coast peoples also pounded the cedar tree's bark, thin branches, and roots into soft weaving material. With this flexible weaving material they made capes, hats, baskets, bags, and mats. The rich environment of the Northwest Coast provided plenty of food—fish, game, and fruit. This abundance of food gave the Northwest peoples more free time to spend on creating art.

The societies of the Pacific Northwest Coast were large, settled communities. Much of their artwork, like totem poles and cedar boxes, could therefore be large. In contrast, the societies of the Plains in the 1700s and 1800s were smaller and very mobile. Therefore, all their art had to be small and easy to carry.

Plains people lived in teepees, which could be taken down and packed up quickly, if needed. Portable arts included many items

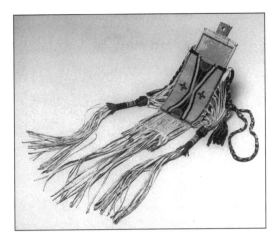

Crow beaded mirror with case, Montana, around 1880.

for personal use: painted shields; soft and sturdy beaded moccasins; fancy headdresses made of feathers and fur; and clothing made of hide and decorated with paint, beads, quills, and hair.

As the Northwest Coast peoples used the cedar tree for their arts, Plains peoples depended on the buffalo. Buffalo hides were used for teepee covers and clothing, the sinew (ligaments or tendons) was used as thread for sewing, and the horn was used for jewelry and carved utensils.

In the cold Arctic areas of Canada and Alaska, life and art both depended on the animal world: caribou, polar bear, salmon, walrus, whale, and seal. Men would carve walrus tusks, caribou antlers, and whale bones into fishing and hunting tools. These tools, such as harpoon heads, knives, and buttons, were both useful and beautiful. Women used animal skins to sew fine and warm clothing. The clothing was designed to protect the wearer from the cold, as well as to please the spirits of the animals who had sacrificed their lives so that humans could eat and stay warm. The shaman, who was the spiritual protector of the people, wore especially fine clothing.

In the southwestern areas of Arizona and New Mexico, the Hopi, Zuni, Pueblo, and other peoples have been farmers for over 1,500 years. Their lives in a fixed place is reflected in many of their arts. Their pueblos are unique multistory apartments, some of which have been in continuous use for hundreds of years. They are made of stone and adobe brick, and the walls are plastered with clay and painted. Clay pottery is made from the earth itself. Clothing was made from cotton and other plants that were grown and harvested. Shell and turquoise jewelry was often traded to groups located hundreds of miles away in every direction.

Pottery of the Casas Grandes people.

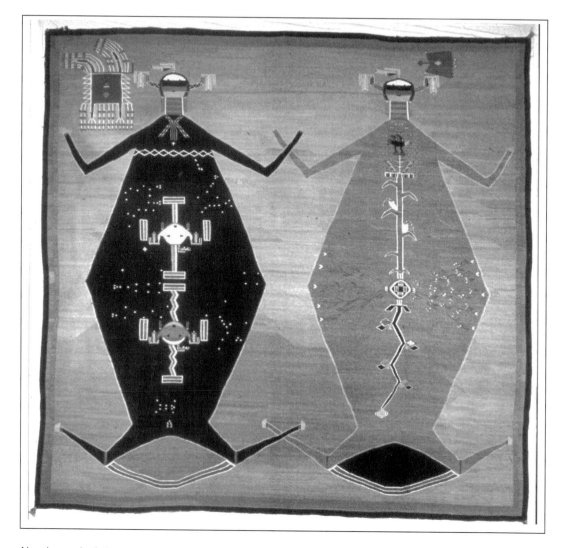

Navajo sandpainting rug woven by Altnabah, early twentieth century.

Art as Sacred

In most Native American cultures, just as life is not divided into the sacred and the secular (or religious and non-religious), neither can art be divided between spiritual and non-spiritual expression. Even in arts where the spiritual meaning is not obvious, it is often a part of the actual making of the object. A look at a Zuni altar, Comanche shield, and Navajo rug illustrate this point.

A Zuni altar is a highly sacred construction. It is decorated with carved and painted figures, feathers, painted pottery bowls for cornmeal, and dry paintings made of sand and crushed minerals. These items are sacred and have power, which is activated when the proper ceremonies are performed over them. Tradition dictates how the parts of the altar are to be made and used, and who is allowed to see them.

A Comanche or Crow shield is a power object as well as an art object. A Plains warrior painted his shield with a particular animal, insect, or any natural thing that appeared to him in a vision. This gave him power and protection in war. Each shield is a highly personal work of art.

In contrast to these two examples, a Navajo rug made for sale to outsiders might not seem to have religious meaning. But for the Navajo all weaving is a sacred activity. In Navajo creation stories, the universe itself was woven on a giant loom by a sacred ancestor named Spider Woman. Spider Woman used the materials of nature as she wove lightning, clouds, rainbows, and sun rays to create the world. Navajo women think about and honor Spider Woman as they use nature's products (wool from sheep, dyes from plants, and their own human creativity) to weave their rugs.

The designs on Navajo rugs are not always obviously religious. However, in the example shown on the facing page, the design represents the sacred arts of medicine and astronomy. Mother Earth is shown as the large figure on the right. Corn, beans, squash, and tobacco, the four most important Native American plants, grow out of her belly. The black figure is Father Sky. In his belly are the sun, moon, and stars (including Orion, the Pleiades, and the Dippers).

Art and Power

In many areas of Native American life, art is used for personal power, or to reveal the power of the group or society. In the 1800s, for example, Sioux men painted pictures showing their brave deeds in war on their buffalo robes, or on the teepees where they lived. In a way, they "owned the rights" to these scenes, for they depicted personal history. A Sioux warrior also owned the rights to any images he discovered through his dreams, which could also be painted on his clothing or teepee. Like any other property, these symbols of power could be bought or inherited by others.

A Cheyenne woman might decorate her clothing with designs sewn of dyed porcupine quills. Like the warrior who decorated his robe and teepee, she owned the rights to these designs. They could be used only by her unless she sold them, or allowed someone else to use them. She gained power and status through her role as a fine artist, just as a Cheyenne man gained honor through his role as a warrior.

Among the Iroquois, a man might dream of a spirit face to aid him in healing. He would then carve a mask of this spirit on the trunk of a basswood tree while the tree was still growing. This "False Face" spirit mask could be used with tobacco in a healing ritual to rid the community or an individual of disease. To the Iroquois, these masks are much more than just art objects. They are believed to have spiritual power. Therefore, they must be handled respectfully, and they are given ritual offerings of cornmeal and tobacco.

A Myth about Art and Power

Some cultures have myths that warn against an artist's improper use of power. These myths demonstrate that it is especially risky for artists to pay so much attention to their art that they don't lead balanced lives. A Tlingit myth from southern Alaska shows that artists must live within society and cooperate with other human beings. (This idea is very different from the non-Native image of the artist who lives alone, totally dedicated to his or her art.)

According to the Tlingit myth, in ancient times there was a young woman who wanted only to perfect the art of weaving, an art that was not common on the Northwest Coast. But she had many male admirers, and their attention made it difficult to devote enough time to her art. Therefore, she decided to live alone in the wilderness.

Raven and Marten (animal heroes in Northwest Coast mythology) found her there, and pretended to be a chief and his son. They got to know her, and the chief asked her to marry his son. She agreed, but only on the condition that they remain in the wilderness so she could continue her weaving undisturbed. Only when the men agreed did she show them her house, which was filled with the most beautiful weavings in the world.

While she slept, Raven and Marten stole all her weavings. They flew back to the communities on the coast and gave her weavings away as gifts to all the women there. From these weavings, women learned to weave the Chilkat Tlingit blankets that would become the most valuable textiles along the Northwest Coast.

This myth serves to caution artists not to seek isolation from their community. Instead of withholding knowledge and skill that would be helpful to others, they should be generous with their art. For a lack of gen-erosity, an artist might lose his or her art as the young Tlingit weaver did.

Learning to Be an Artist

Among many Native American societies, people report that they get ideas for art through their dreams. A Sioux woman, for example, may dream of a new way to design her pattern of colored beads. She may even dream of the spirit of Double Woman, the patron of Sioux beadworkers. It is said that if a woman dreams of Double Woman, she will be an extraordinary artist.

In some tribes, all people are considered to be artistic and are responsible for making and decorating their own goods. In these societies people recognized as having more skill than others may be asked to make cere-monial objects or special gifts. Children learn to create art from their parents or other adults.

In other societies, making art is consid-ered a special job. To become an artist, one must learn from an expert. For example, young Kwakiutl or Tlingit boys become apprentices to a master artist who teach them to carve. An apprentice's first jobs might be simple: to keep the fire going, sharpen tools, or grind up minerals that give the paint its colors. As he gets older, the apprentice will be given more responsibility. He might, for instance, be allowed to remove the bark from the piece of log and rough out the face of the mask. The finishing work is then done by the master artist. A more advanced apprentice might work as the "other side man." The master carver would plan out a totem pole design and carve the right side, while the apprentice would copy the master's work on the "other side."

Signing Artworks

Before the mid-1900s, most Native American art was unsigned. Most collectors did not bother to find out who had created the art. Therefore, when visitors to museums see these objects, they may not realize that they were created by individual artists with unique styles and ideas.

Within the tribe, however, signing works of art was not necessary. Tribes are small communities, and everyone in the tribe knew and recognized the special style of a particular artist. For example, a weaver may be recognized by her special way of finishing off the edge of her blanket.

In some areas in the early 1900s, artists were encouraged by non-Natives to sign their works. Signing was encouraged because this had been the custom in European and American art since the Renaissance (about the 1500s). For example, in the 1920s San Ildefonso Pueblo potter Maria Martinez was urged to sign the bottoms of her famous blackware pots because buyers would pay more for her work than for the work of others. For the Pueblo, however, this was a problem because they valued balance, cooperation, and group harmony more than individual achievement. To keep jealousies and unfairness to a minimum, over a period of 20 years Maria signed her name to pots that were made and painted by others. She also polished and signed pots that other women had formed. To outsiders, this may seem to be dishonest. But to the Pueblo it was a way for other artists to share in the high prices brought by the fame of Maria Martinez. It was also a way to keep relationships within the group running smoothly.

Maria Martinez, potter of San Ildefonso Pueblo, New Mexico, and her blackware designs, 1940s.

Ceremonies, Rituals, Festivals, Music, and Dance

In every American Indian society, the visual arts (textiles, pottery, painting, photography, architecture, sculpture) are linked to the arts of music, dance, festivals, and ceremonies. Artistic objects are created and used for their power. Masks, dance costumes, carved rattles, and other ceremonial items add to the power and beauty of any ceremony.

Indian music and dance occur everywhere in North America: on large reservations like the Navajo, on small California rancherias like Morongo, in big cities like Los Angeles, in rural areas like the mountains of North Carolina, and at sacred places like Canyon de Chelly in Arizona.

Music and Musical Instruments

In Indian music, the voice is the most important instrument. Most songs are performed in native languages. Melodies are sung with a background of voices that add texture and body to the song. Most are accompanied by a rattle or drum, or both.

The water drum is unique to North America. It is made from a small container of wood, pottery, or metal, which is partially filled with water for tuning. It is covered with a dampened soft hide stretched tight and beaten with a hard stick by only one person at a time. Water drums are used by eastern Indians, the Apache and Navajo, and members of the Native American Church.

Various types of rattles or scrapers are often used to add texture to the music. One type is the vessel rattle, a container filled with pebbles or fruit seeds. It may be played by lead or backup singers, dancers, or by people who are singing and dancing at the same time. Rattles may be made of many different materials, including wood, baskets, gourds, bark, moose feet, clay, metal, turtle shells, cow horns, copper, coconut shells, and buffalo tails. Another type of rattle is strung and fastened to sticks, hoops, or textiles. These are held or attached to the bodies or clothing of dancers. They may be made from bird beaks, cocoons, deer hooves, tin cans, turtle shells, sea shells, or metal cones. Less common instruments are scrapers, wooden box drums, flutes, whistles, fiddles, musical bows, and clapping sticks.

The most common forms of music among Native Americans are song cycles and simple short songs repeated many times. Songs vary according to tribe and geographic area. Even without knowing a particular song, a knowledgeable listener can usually tell the tribe or area the song came from. Clues may be the style and rhythm of the melody, or the way instruments are used.

The most common form of song is the Plains Indian powwow, or intertribal, song. It features a lead singer and a chorus. The lead singer will start with one phrase, sung as high as possible. The chorus members, who are singing and drumming, answer him by repeating that phrase, although changing it slightly. Then all sing the melody together. This is repeated in a variety of patterns with the pitch getting lower and lower each time. The male dancers wear loud ankle bells. Some blow whistles to show their delight with the singers and to ask for a repetition. The "pulsation" or quivering of the voices enhances the sound and helps to create the song's style.

The music that is best known to the public is from ceremonies and social occasions that are not private. Private songs—such as those for medicine and healing, prayer, hunting, performing magic, courtships (not necessarily familiar to outsiders)—are important art forms.

The way singers and dancers work together, the ceremonial clothing they wear, the face and body paint used, the words and instruments used, the structure of the songs—all are related to the group's traditions and ways of looking at the world. A look at the Cherokee will illustrate this. If the words to a Cherokee song mention east, north, west, and south in that order, the

Dene jigging, Midway Lake Gwichin Music Festival, Fort McPherson, Northwest Territory, 1988.

dancers probably start in the east and move counterclockwise throughout the dance. If colors are mentioned, they are probably in a similar order: red (representing east), blue (north), black (west), and white (south). Other tribes may have different ways of organizing their ceremonies based on how they look at the world.

Traditional songs, passed down through generations, are cherished by many people. However, some people do make changes to the music, adding different instruments or perhaps adding English words. Sometimes popular American songs inspire Indian composers, and their words or melodies find a place in modern Indian music. New songs

are composed every year and spread across the nation during powwow season (from Memorial Day to Labor Day in the United States).

Dance

Dance, like other music forms, is rarely a solo event in Native American traditions. Rather than showing the skill of an individual, Indian dances usually show established patterns and movements. Some dances have a leader and chorus, while in others the dancers act together. Some dances feature soloists, but few give individual dancers the freedom to show off. This is because group dances stem from the value Native Ameri-

Masked dancers participating in a Kwakiutl winter ceremonial.

cans place on cooperation and group effort. Some individual expression is allowed in Plains dances, but most Pueblo dances have strict rules and require all to move as one, interrupted from time to time only by the antics of a ritual clown.

Many traditional dances have spiritual origins and are tied to celebrations of the seasons or the cycles of life. The dances vary from tribe to tribe, and from region to region, and the ceremonies reflect local customs and ways of life. For example, the use of leaders and followers, unison action (acting as one), the cooperation of individuals who assume different roles, and the ideal of several generations working together all may be reflected in dance.

Indian dancers use small movements and stay close to the earth, for both religious and practical reasons. From a practical standpoint, they take small steps to save their energy because some dances may last all day or all night. Or there may be limited space in which to dance, or a large number of dancers. In dances like the Creek Buffalo Dance and the Taos Eagle Dance, dancers imitate animals. The work of hunting, fishing, planting, harvesting, warfare, or other activities may also be represented in dance. The dancers stay close to the earth, just as these activities are done close to the earth.

Dancers often move in circles, either clockwise or counterclockwise, depending on how they view the world and the directions. Most Plains and urban Indian dances, such as powwows, use clockwise patterns, while most Eastern tribes dance in a counterclockwise pattern. Many Navajo social dances allow the dancers to alternate directions for different songs.

Musical Games

Most games played by Native Americans include music, and sometimes dance. The most popular games are hand games or stick games. These are guessing games, and are found almost everywhere in North America. In these games, the players sing while hiding an object or the mark on a stick. The members of the other team try to guess the location of the object or mark, and then it is their turn to sing and hide. Each team scores points for fooling its opponents, and the first team to reach a certain total of points wins the game. Each team has lucky songs, and the game cannot exist without the songs.

Usually the songs are easy to sing, with short phrases so the players can concentrate on guessing. Among some tribes, such as in the Northwest Coast, stick game songs have complicated rhythms and multipart singing. Among some groups, such as the Washoe and Pomo in central California, men and women play entirely separate games.

Arctic peoples have other musical games. These include vocal contests between two women at a time (on Baffin Island), and the insult-singing contests (to settle differences of opinion) of the Netsilik.

In the southeastern United States, the Cherokee, Creek, Choctaw, and Seminole play ceremonial stickball games, very similar to lacrosse. Songs and dances are performed both before and after the games.

Women singers sing encouraging words for their own teams and insults against the opposing teams. Today these games often leave out many of the songs, dances, and ceremonial aspects when they are played only "for show."

Peyote Music

The peyote religion and music of the Native American Church are widespread throughout North America. Peyote music is so popular that dozens of recordings of it have been released by the two major Indian record companies, Indian House and Canyon.

In general, peyote music is fast and uses a ceremonial water drum and rattle to accompany the singers. The drum is played with a driving pulse; worshippers take turns playing it as they pass it clockwise around a sacred area containing fire, sage, a peyote button, water, and cedar. At special times during the ceremony a whistle made of eagle bone is blown outside in the four directions.

Powwows

Like other Americans, Native Americans sing and dance to whatever kind of music they enjoy, for the most part saving traditional music for special occasions. The Indian powwow is just such an occasion. The main activity of a powwow is singing and dancing, and the singers and dancers at powwows usually come from many different tribes. Feasting, giveaways, arts and crafts sales, raffles, and the crowning of a princess may also be included.

At powwows the singers generally perform Plains Indian music—northern, southern, or both. Music and dance from a specific region or tribe may be performed also. Many different types of dances may be included in a powwow, including Gourd Dances, War Dances, Grass Dances, and Round Dances.

Various social and couples dances, such as the Oklahoma Two-Step, Rabbit Dance, Snake Dance, and Owl Dance may be part of the powwow. These social dances offer the audience a chance to participate freely, without having to meet the formal requirements for the more serious dances. Special dances such as the Navajo Ribbon Dance (a mirror-image dance by one or two sets of partners) or the Swan Dance (an imitation of the bird) may also be performed at a powwow.

In recent years, the sponsors of powwows have held contests to attract the best singers and dancers to their events. Leaders choose the head singers and dancers not only for their skill and knowledge, but for their standing in the community and their network of family and friends. If the powwow leaders have status and the respect of the community, other good singers and dancers will join to show their support.

Drums, or groups of Indian men singers, have been formed all across the United States. The purpose of these drums is to perform at powwows or other gatherings. But one of the main benefits is that men from different tribes meet together on a weekly or monthly basis to practice and to socialize.

In the past, most young women participated only in dancing, or doing beadwork or other crafts. Recently, however, women have taken roles as singers or composers. Some have even joined male drums, or formed their own female drums.

After powwows, "Forty-nine" dances may be held. These are social dances performed mostly by young people. They may last all night. The dress is casual, and the dances and songs are done mostly for fun. The songs may be about love, sweethearts, or life's everyday problems. Many young Native Americans have never experienced traditional Indian life. They rely on powwows and other community activities to learn about Native traditions and to help define their identity as Indians.

22

Native American Literature

FACT FOCUS

- Native American poetry usually does not use rhyme or meter. Because it comes from oral traditions, it often uses sequence and tone to convey its meaning.
- The Pulitzer Prize for literature was awarded to American Indian writer N. Scott Momaday for his novel *House Made of Dawn*.
- Young Lakota men composed flute songs to get the attention of their sweethearts.
- Until the twentieth century very few autobiographies were written down by Native Americans. Instead, Indians told their life stories to others who wrote them down. These are called "as told to" stories.
- The first novel by an American Indian woman, *Cogewea, the Halfblood* (1927), by Mourning Dove, is about a young Native American woman trying to decide whether to marry a non-Native or a half-Native man.

Oral literature, or literature that is spoken rather than written down, can take many forms. In traditional Native American cultures, stories, myths, legends, ritual dramas, prayers, chants, songs, speeches, anecdotes (very brief stories), and even jokes are all forms of oral literature.

For thousands of years, traditional Native North American literature was expressed only orally, so it can be difficult for a person outside of a particular Native culture to gain access to its literature. But many Indian cultures painted, carved, or etched pictorial stories into rocks, animal hides, and other materials. **Petroglyphs,** stories or events related through pictures carved into rock, have been found throughout North America. [Also see Arts chapter.]

Some of the ancient oral literature of Native American cultures has been put into print after enjoying a long life among a people. These drawn, carved, or written pieces are only a sample of the rich and varied forms of oral literature that have been passed down through countless generations. Meanwhile, oral literature continues to enrich the

Early American Indians often recorded histories and stories on rocks and cliffs at sacred sites. The above petroglyphs were found in San Gabriel Canyon in Southern California.

lives of many Native American peoples, especially as they revive the practice of their traditional ceremonies and customs.

In traditional Native cultures, elders told stories, myths, and legends. Ceremonies and songs were performed among the people. Oral literature served religious, entertainment, and educational purposes, often at the same time. In particular, the young people of the tribe were educated in this way. They learned the religion, moral values, history, artistic values, humor, and music of their tribe.

More and more traditional literature has been written down in recent times as Native American storytellers and poets work to preserve their cultures. These writers also express and record their own modern experiences, either in English or sometimes in Native American languages.

Creation Myths

As in many other cultures, **creation myths** (sacred stories that explain how the world was created) are a cornerstone in many

Northwest Coast dancers embodied spiritual beings and reenacted creation histories and traditional stories.

Native American peoples' view of the world. They often help explain a people's history in a particular place and show the relationship between human beings and the environment.

In North America, there are at least three common types of creation myths. One is the Earth-Diver Myth, in which the world is covered by water. In nearly every form of this myth, an animal dives down into the water and brings up mud or earth to begin the world. He succeeds only after three companions before him have failed. The second type of creation story is the Emergence Myth, in which humans, animals, and plants live in a cave below the world. They emerge into the sun by flying up, or by climbing a reed, tree, or root. A third type of creation myth is the Two Creators Myth, in which two god-like beings create the world in competition with one another. [Also see Religion chapter.]

Trickster Stories and Myths

Tricksters are powerful, god-like beings who can change the world or interfere, often comically, in the lives of men. Trickster stories are common among many Native groups. The Trickster takes many different forms: Coyote in the Southwest, Ikhtomi Spider in the High Plains, Hare in the Great Lakes and Southeast, Raven in the Northwest, and Jay or Wolverine in parts of Canada.

Depending on the tribe's traditions, stories about these characters may be used to teach proper behavior to children, to instruct

"COYOTE LAYS DOWN THE LAW"

It was said,
"Let the river flow downstream on one side,
and upstream on the other side.
Let it be so."
And so it was agreed.
Whenever they traveled downstream,
the boat would drift downstream.
But they would travel back upriver on the other side.
They'd drift upstream, too.
It was flowing upriver, that water was.

And then Coyote said, "No,
let it not be that way.
Let it all flow downriver.
Let the young husbands push their way up there,
when they travel upstream."
But then it was said,
"When women carry their packbaskets uphill,
then uphill they put wood into them,
they make basketloads.
And then the women start back home.
And they just leave them there, those basketloads.
And they said,
"They'll just walk home, those basketloads will."

And then Coyote said, "No, don't!
Let the young wives just carry the loads."
So that's the way it is nowadays.
Now they can't walk any more, those basketloads.

or inspire adults, or to entertain through humor. Trickster tales may also present a culture hero who saves the people or makes the world better by his brave acts. They may tell how the universe came to be, or why things are as they are.

"Coyote Lays Down the Law" (see box on this page) is a short poem from the Karuk of northwestern California. It is an example of a Trickster story, as well as an example of Native American poetry. The main character is Coyote, a divine Trickster, who stars in hundreds of stories told by the tribes of western North America. Like other tricksters, Coyote interferes with the workings of the natural world and makes peoples' lives more difficult.

The poem has two acts, each made up of two scenes. In the first scene, the primeval world is described with the river flowing

Stories and legends were often reenacted through dances. Here the American Indian Dance Theatre performs an Eagle Dance.

two ways. In the second scene, Coyote tampers with the river, making it much harder for the men to go upstream. In the next scene, women's baskets full of wood carry themselves home. In the final scene, Coyote again tampers, making the women's work much more difficult.

Unlike European or English poetry, the poetry of American Indian cultures usually does not use rhyme or meter (a rhythm, or a pattern of beats). However, it is frequently organized in lines and sequences. As the myth is spoken or read, the words, sounds, structure, pauses, and tone of voice all combine to create a poetic effect.

A myth such as "Coyote Lays Down the Law" has much more meaning when told within a Native American culture than it does when one simply reads it. Most traditional Native American stories come to life through a group's shared history, culture, and beliefs, as well as through the listener's personal history. Like stories in any other culture, traditional stories are understood as part of a network of stories all members of the group know and cherish.

Legends and Coup Stories

Native American legends differ from myths in that they describe an actual event that happened long ago and has passed from generation to generation through storytelling. Over time these stories may become exaggerated and they begin to take on special meanings within the understanding of the group. A non-Native example is the story of Daniel Boone, an American folk hero who supposedly killed a bear with his bare hands. Many Native American legends involve some form of the Trickster figure. Legends are told to present a culture hero who makes the world better through his or her brave acts, or to explain how the world came to be as we know it.

Coup (pronounced "koo," a sudden, brilliant action or clever move) stories usually tell of great feats of strength, bravery, and heroism. When Plains warriors tell of their own brave deeds in battle, they too play the part of culture heroes, but on a smaller scale than legendary figures. Other warriors who witnessed the event are usually there when the story is told to swear that the teller's story is true.

Rituals, Songs, and Chants

Songs and chants are other forms of oral literature that are often recorded. Some are generations old; others are composed for just one occasion and may or may not continue to be used. Songs created for social occasions are sometimes called "forty-nines" and may be in the native language, or English, or both.

Around the turn of the twentieth century, there was much concern that American Indian cultures were dying out. Scholars made great efforts to record the Native American literary materials. Early collections of Indian literature recorded the spoken parts of Native American rituals. Some of these collections reveal sacred tribal information that the tribe did not wish to be published. Taken out of context, the spoken parts of rituals will not mean the same thing to a non-Indian as they mean to a member of the tribe.

On the other hand, some tribes, such as the Iroquois, gladly share their ceremonies with audiences outside their group.

Among the Lakota, young men at one time composed flute songs in order to court the young women they wanted to marry. Usually a medicine man would help them write the songs. The young man would sit on a hill behind the young woman's teepee and play the song, which might contain words she had spoken. If she wanted nothing to do with him, she would ignore him and his song. If she were interested in him, she might come out with an older female relative (such as a sister or aunt) to listen to the song. Flute songs are rarely used in courtship today.

Speeches

Oratory, or speech-making, is one of the most widely known forms of Native oral literature. Native American cultures have always placed a high value upon public-speaking abilities. Chief Sealth (also known as Chief Seattle, after whom the city in Washington state is named), a Suquamish who lived from 1786 to 1866, was one well-known orator. One of Chief Sealth's speeches is often quoted by many different groups for its environmental message that all people, plants, and animals on earth are related.

In 1772, Samson Occom (a Mohegan) published his *Sermon Preached at the Execution of Moses Paul*. This was the first time a Native American who could read and write controlled the publication and presentation of his speech. The sermon, criticizing non-Natives for supplying alcohol to Native peoples, was very popular in its day. Peter Nabokov's *Native American Testimony: A Chronicle of Indian-White Relations from Prophecy to the Present, 1492-1992*, contains many fine examples of American Indian speeches, as well as excerpts from autobiographies.

Life Histories and Autobiographies

Many early Native American writers wished to record the histories, religious beliefs, and political causes of their people. In the late 1700s and the 1800s, Samson Occom, William Apes, David Cusick, George Copway, Peter Jones, and others wrote such works. Native American autobiography is unique because over 80 percent has been collected and edited by non-Native people. One reason for this was the lack of **literacy** (ability to read and write) among Native peoples at the time. Another reason is that, until very recently, American Indian autobiography was written mostly for non-Native audiences. Many Native American individuals, who might be quite well known within their tribes, would find it odd to describe their lives and personal struggles for publication. They have many stories about themselves to share with one another, but do not tend to focus on their individuality as much as people from other cultures do. Tribal people usually define themselves more as a part of the whole community, so autobiography is a literary form that does not fit very well with their view of themselves.

A Son of the Forest, written by William Apes in 1829, is the earliest known autobiography in English by a Native American. Apes had converted to Christianity after many sad years as a foster child. He wrote about the abuses he and other American Indian people suffered at the hands of Europeans, and about his new faith. George Copway's *Life, History, and Travels of Kah-ge-ga-gah-bowh* was

Sarah Winnemucca Hopkins.

a popular book, published in 1847 and reprinted six times in its first year.

The first autobiography by an American Indian woman was *Life among the Piutes* [sic], by Sarah Winnemucca Hopkins. She spoke out strongly against the way the Paiutes were treated by the Indian agents and non-Native settlers. Hopkins also described the virtues of her people's traditional ways and the need for government reform to protect the Paiutes and other tribes. Throughout most of her life, she acted as a liaison between her people and non-Native officials.

Charles Eastman, a Santee Sioux, wrote

two autobiographies, *Indian Boyhood* (1902) and *From Deep Woods to Civilization* (1916). He also wrote many books on Dakota culture. Eastman's autobiographies describe his life before contact with non-Indians at age 15, as well as his education and career. He was a YMCA and Boy Scout leader and organizer, a public lecturer and writer, and a medical doctor on two reservations. He was the physician at the Pine Ridge reservation at the time of the Wounded Knee Massacre in 1890, when the U.S. Cavalry killed more than 300 Sioux, mostly unarmed women and children, and he provided a valuable historical record of that disaster. Throughout his life he worked to further the causes of American Indians. Eastman spent over 20 years trying to restore the treaty rights of his people.

Luther Standing Bear, a Lakota, began writing after he had traveled with Buffalo Bill's Wild West Show, acted in movies, and engaged in political activities to help American Indians. *Land of the Spotted Eagle,* published in 1933, is probably the best known of his three autobiographical works. Standing Bear also wrote a children's book, *My Indian Boyhood.* Francis LaFlesche's *The Middle Five* is also about life as a young Native American. This book, written in 1900, tells the moving and tragic story of the author's years in a Presbyterian boarding school.

"As told to" stories form a special category of American Indian autobiography. These are Native life stories written with the help of others. The first to appear was *Black Hawk, an Autobiography,* recorded by Antoine Le Claire. This great war chief's story was published in 1833. Black Hawk wanted his side of the Black Hawk War of 1832 to be known, since all the newspaper accounts had ignored the injustices done to his Sauk people.

Since *Black Hawk* a number of "as told to" autobiographies have been published. Some of the best-known are *Crashing Thunder,* by Blowsnake, as told to Paul Radin; *Mountain Wolf Woman,* by herself (as told to Nancy Lurie); *Sun Chief,* by Don Talayesva (Leo Simmons); *Papago Woman,* by Maria Chona (Ruth Underhill); and *Cheyenne Memories* (1967), by John Stands in Timber (Margot Liberty). In *Life Lived Like a Story* (1990), three Alaska Native women told their stories to writer Julie Cruikshank.

Many of the recorders of Native American autobiography were careful to record their subjects' lives exactly as they were told to them and in the order that they were told. Others, however, attempted to order the sequences of events in the way European-based cultures are used to reading them, beginning with childhood, ending with old age. In one of the most famous "as told to" biographies, *Black Elk Speaks* (1932), writer John G. Neihardt presented the words of the Oglala Sioux warrior and medicine man, but also Neihardt's own poetic and powerful understanding of Black Elk's vision.

Black Elk witnessed the Battle of Little Big Horn as a boy of 13. Many years later he experienced the massacre of Indians at Wounded Knee. Throughout his life his people were pushed into smaller and more regulated living areas. *Black Elk Speaks* tells of these events, but Black Elk's intent was to express the meaning of all life that had been presented to him in several visions.

Many feel that *Black Elk Speaks* ranks among the most important holy books of the

BLACK ELK INTRODUCES HIS STORY IN *BLACK ELK SPEAKS*

This, then, is not the tale of a great hunter or of a great warrior, or of a great traveler, although I have made much meat in my time and fought for my people both as boy and man, and have gone far and seen strange lands and men. So also have many others done, and better than I. These things I shall remember by the way, and often they may seem to be the very tale itself, as I was living them in happiness and sorrow. But now that I can see it all as from a lonely hill top, I know it was the story of a mighty vision given to a man too weak to use it; of a holy tree that should have flourished in a people's heart with flowers and singing birds, and now is withered; and of a people's dream that died in bloody snow. But if the vision was true and mighty, as I know, it is true and mighty yet; for such things are of the spirit, and it is in the darkness of their eyes that men get lost.

John Rollin Ridge

world. A famous psychologist, Carl Jung, saw in it many similarities to the life stories of other religious figures. Jung's interest in the book helped it to be republished in 1959. Writer Vine Deloria, Jr., called *Black Elk Speaks* a "veritable Indian Bible" for youth of the 1960s and 1970s because it shows the beauty and value in traditional Native American religion.

More autobiographies include *Lakota Woman,* by Mary Crow Dog. This is the story of a young woman who was an activist in AIM (American Indian Movement, a group organized to promote Native American rights and values) of the 1970s. Mary Crow Dog describes her life as the wife of a medicine man and as a person of mixed-blood in the Indian world. *Interior Landscapes* (1990) by Gerald Vizenor and *Black Eagle Child: The Facepaint Narratives*

(1992) by Ray A. Young Bear are two other compelling autobiographies.

Fiction and Poetry

The first American Indian novel, *Life and Adventures of Joaquin Murieta,* was written in 1854 by John Rollin Ridge, a Cherokee. Ridge moved to California after his tribe was removed to Oklahoma during the 1830s. His father and brother were murdered because they favored removal. Ridge became a newspaperman and eventually owned his own newspaper. In his novel, the hero is an outlaw with a heart, who avenges the downtrodden as he goes from one wild adventure to another.

The Singing Spirit is a book of early Native American short stories collected by Bernd C. Peyer and published in 1989. The authors of these stories, most of whom were born in the 1870s, include Gertrude Bonnis, Francis and Suzette LaFlesche, Alexander Posey, Charles Eastman, D'Arcy McNickle, and Pauline Johnson.

The first novel by an American Indian woman was *Cogewea, the Halfblood* (1927), by Mourning Dove. It is about a young Native American woman trying to decide whether to marry a non-Native or a half-Native man. She finally chooses the man with Indian blood and affirms her culture. The theme of being caught between two worlds and having to choose, and the problems faced by people of mixed heritage in American society, have been taken up by other writers throughout the 1900s.

In the early 1970s, American Indian writers began producing fiction and poetry as never before. This movement found its first voice in N. Scott Momaday, whose novel *House Made of Dawn* (1968) won the Pulitzer Prize for literature. Vine Deloria's *Custer Died for Your Sins* (1969) was published during the Indian occupation of the abandoned prison on Alcatraz Island in San Francisco Bay, a protest against the living conditions on most reservations. The book caused a tremendous stir in the public imagination. Dee Brown's *Bury My Heart at Wounded Knee,* which became a best-seller in 1972, tells the Native American side of the story of the settling of the American West.

Since then, many Native American writers of fiction and poetry have become widely known and read. James Welch, Duane Niatum, Gery Hobson, Leslie Silko, Simon Ortiz, Louise Erdrich, Paula Gunn Allen, Wendy Rose, Joy Harjo, Ray A. Young Bear, Beth Brant, and Gerald Vizenor are all contemporary Native American writers. Some of the main themes that appear in their works are **alienation** (feeling set apart from society, one's own identity, or one's roots), loss, cultural change, control of traditional Native American cultures, women's issues and roles, and the conflict between Native and non-Native ways.

New Native American writers and their works emerge every day. Luci Tapahonso, Nia Francisco, and Rex Lee Jim are all Navajo who write bilingual works (in two languages) and include Native songs in their works. Playwrights like Hanay Geiogamah and William S. Yellow Robe, Jr., produce plays that are becoming known internationally. As a "new" field within American literature, Native American literature will continue to grow and to change the way America sees itself.

23

Media

FACT FOCUS

- In the Canadian Arctic, the Inuit, frustrated with the invasion of English-language television in their society, created the Inuit Broadcasting Corporation, through which they broadcast Inuit-language programs.
- The Native American Public Broadcasting Consortium (NAPBC) was formed in Lincoln, Nebraska, in the early 1980s to support and encourage Native work in television, video, and films. Its members have produced over 250 original works.
- In *Return of the Country*, an independent film made by Bob Hicks, a Creek-Seminole, Indians discover America and promptly establish a Bureau of Caucasian Affairs. Non-Indian children are forced to abandon the English language, shed their European-style dress, and shun the Christian religion.
- Many Native American plays and films blend contemporary issues with traditional myths and legends.
- The first all-Indian professional acting company, called the American Indian (later Native American) Theatre Ensemble, was founded in the 1970s in New York City.

In the past, Indian communicators and artists—storytellers, musical composers, poets, oral historians, and performing artists—worked in a very personal mode. Communicators were not set apart from the tribe in any special sense. Their place was with their people. They drew inspiration from their people and created art for them with a specific purpose. There was very little "art for art's sake."

Beginning in the 1960s, Native Americans, like all Americans, found themselves in the midst of what has been called "the Media Age." From the 1960s to the present, American culture has been transformed by the rapid development of all the **media**—television, radio, films, and printed matter. The media have made masses of information available to people and play an ever increasing role in shaping and defining reality for millions. For tribal people, the media offer special challenges and opportunities.

Richard La Course is a Yakima tribal journalist and historian who founded the

American Indian Press Association in the early 1970s. In 1972, La Course said:

> In more secure times than these, everything the Indian individual needed to know for self-definition and for tribal definition was made available with the luxury and times of years. For children, winters were for stories. For all, summer was for dances, and feasts were held in the early fall. In the different tribal orders of time, the pace of growth and the pace of understanding was assured. But in many tribal sectors today ... much of the knowledge, the definition of Indian life borne in the life of one's own grandfather and grandmother, is vanishing with time and death. It is timely and mandatory to seek avenues not to replace those traditional modes of communication, but rather to restore and enhance them toward a truly Indian future.

The challenge, in other words, is for Native Americans to use the media to strengthen tribal heritage and pride. In 1993, there were nearly two million Native Americans belonging to 427 tribes. Many of the leaders of these tribes share a strong belief that the media form a powerful tool that can help them achieve their goals. Some of these goals are to protect their lands and natural resources; improve tribal economies and businesses; develop housing, education, and health programs; and to preserve their traditional culture.

Native American communicators and artists have joined together to form organizations to support their goals. The American Indian Press Association was founded in Washington, D.C., in the 1970s. It worked

Part of the cast of all-Native American dancers and musicians with the American Indian Dance Theatre.

to gather and distribute news and information to dozens of reservation and community newspapers across Indian Country. It was succeeded by the Native American Journalists' Association, which represents over 150 publications and nearly one million readers.

To the far north in the Canadian Arctic is the home of the Inuit Broadcasting Corporation (IBC). The IBC is a model for Native **broadcasters** all over the world. The Inuit were frustrated with the invasion of English-language television in their society. They responded by creating their own broadcasting center, and producing programs entirely in the Inuit language. The

A highlight of the American Indian Dance Theatre performance is the Women's Fancy Shawl Dance.

IBC's history is told in a film, *Starting Fire with Gunpowder* (1991).

In the 1970s, the American Indian Theatre Ensemble (later called the Native American Theatre Ensemble) was founded in New York City. It was the first professional acting company composed entirely of Indian performers. In the years that followed, more than a dozen other Indian theatres were established across the United States. Over one hundred original plays, musicals, and other theatrical works have been produced by these groups. A new generation of actors, writers, directors, producers, and technicians is emerging from this theater movement.

During the 1980s, Native theater in Canada was especially active. Several performing arts groups were formed, including Native Earth Performing Arts Company in Toronto and De-Bah-Jeh-Mu-Jig Theatre on Manitoulin Island. Many troupes, such as the Inuit Company Tununiq Theatre, perform works that target specific social problems like wife-beating or child abuse. All the Native plays blend the traditional with contemporary. A variety of themes appear in these works, including women's issues and non-Native perceptions of Native people. Tribal myths and legends are often woven into the plays.

In 1983, the American Indian Registry

A scene from the play *Dry Lips Oughta Move to Kapuskasing* (1989) by Tomson Highway, which explores sexism among Native men. Native Earth Performing Arts, Inc., Toronto, Canada.

for the Performing Arts was established to support American Indian actors, directors, producers, and others working in Hollywood. The Native American Public Broadcasting Consortium (NAPBC) was formed in Lincoln, Nebraska, in the early 1980s to support and encourage Native work in television, video, and films. Its members have produced over 250 original works. The NAPBC also strongly supports American Indian television programming on public television stations across the country, and addresses tribal and cultural concerns.

As an outgrowth of the work of the NAPBC, in 1990, the American Indian Pro-

ducers Group was formed to promote Native self-determination within the media industry. One of this group's main goals is to produce "quality and culturally appropriate productions involving Native Americans....We say our people deserve their inherent right to dignified and respectful presentation."

Indians in Film and Theatre

The Image of Native Americans in Film and Theatre

In film and theater, American Indians have usually been portrayed in one of two ways—as either "noble savages" (proud,

Southern Men's Traditional Dance. Morgan Tosee, a member of the Comanche tribe of Oklahoma, is a champion Southern Men's Traditional dancer with the American Indian Dance Theatre.

independent, and honorable) or "blood-thirsty savages" (attacking and scalping innocent white settlers). Both of these **images** came from the viewpoint of the non-Natives who wrote and produced the films and plays. Many Indian people do not like these images because Hollywood films often stereotype Indian characters without giving a reasonable understanding of Indian cultures. Indians believe that these works have always indicated more about the non-Natives' viewpoint than they have about the realities of Native American people. Increasingly, however, Native playwrights

and film producers offer new **perspectives** on Indian culture. These works, based on Indian perspectives, create a much different image of Native Americans. Native Americans also hope to promote the Native viewpoint even in contemporary works produced by non-Natives. They have been successful to varying degrees.

Throughout the years, non-Indian playwrights, filmmakers, and performers have created countless works about Indian people, which often bear little resemblance to the people they claim to describe. North American Indians were represented in the

Urban Indians picketing Warner Brothers in the making of the movie *They Died with Their Boots On.*

first play performed in North America. Entitled *The Theatre of Neptume,* it was written in 1606 and performed in present-day Nova Scotia, Canada. Natives were played by Frenchmen in Indian costume, and their speeches were artificial and unnatural. Their main duty in the play was to welcome the new settlers, who were shown as a much-needed "civilizing influence."

In *Native Americans as Shown on the Stage, 1753-1916,* Eugene Jones suggests that the representation of Indians was greatly affected by the needs of the non-Native people. For example, in the early 1800s, Natives were portrayed as noble and non-threatening to colonial power, as in *She Would Be a Soldier* (1819). This play showed Indians helping the United States fight the War of 1812.

From 1830 to 1840, many settlers moved westward and Native peoples were removed from valuable lands. This sparked anxiety in the non-Natives, and the belief that Natives were "a dying race" helped relieve the tension. When Native resistance to removal resulted in the Plains Wars of the 1870s, relations between settlers and Indians had worsened. Plays of this time showed Indians to be worthless savages who deserved to be killed by the superior settlers. The racism of this period is shown in *The Red Right Hand,* a popular play in 1876. In it, "Buffalo Bill" Cody tears off an Indian's scalp, presents it to the audience, and shouts: "The first scalp for Custer!"

One of the first films to depict Indians was *The Sioux Ghost Dance* made in 1894 by the (Thomas) Edison Studios. This short silent film showed five Sioux Indians dressed in breechcloth and headfeathers, beating on drums and dancing on a stage. Early films showed Indians in a variety of roles, mostly as noble or not-so-noble savages. Occasionally, films showed cultural aspects of Native life, and some dealt with issues such as Indian and non-Indian marriages, racism, or separation from one's culture. Several films demonstrated the dilemma of the educated Indian who is not accepted either by his own tribe or by American society. Other films condemned U.S. policies toward Indians, notably *The Vanishing American* in 1925.

In the 1930s, many "B Westerns" were made. These were low budget cowboy pictures with simple "good guy versus bad guy" plots. Because they were low budget,

Will Sampson (Creek) and Jack Nicholson starred in the hit movie *One Flew Over the Cuckoo's Nest,* 1975.

WORDS TO KNOW

broadcast: to make public through radio or television.

image: a mental picture or idea held in common by a social group. When Hollywood movies repeatedly portray Indians in a particular way, the American public may form an inaccurate *image* of what life may be like for the many tribes of American Indians. [Also see definition in Art chapter.]

media: sources, such as television, radio, theater, films, newspapers, magazines, and other printed matter, through which information, entertainment, and other popular forms of mass communication reach audiences.

perspective: the viewpoint from which something is seen; the background or position from which a subject is mentally viewed or considered.

stereotype: a mental *image* held in common by a group of people that represents an oversimplified or prejudiced viewpoint.

costly scenes of Indian attacks or buffalo stampedes were used over and over again. Non-Indians in make-up were used as extras. Movie serials such as *Last of the Mohicans* 1932) and *Lone Ranger* (1938) made the image of the Indian as either an ally or a villain popular. *The Lone Ranger* featured Thunder Cloud (a Cherokee) as the screen's first Tonto. Jay Silverheels, a Mohawk Indian, portrayed Tonto in the 1950s TV series, and Michael Horse played Tonto in the recent *Legend of the Lone Ranger* (1981).

By the mid-1930s, the cowboy became the benevolent hero of the movies, as he drove Indians from the Plains and made the frontier safe for settlers. *Stagecoach* (1939) showed Apaches being mowed down like blades of grass. This and many other westerns that cast Indians as unwelcome aliens in their own land left an indelible mark on the American mind.

When World War II broke out in Europe in the early 1940s, the U.S. War Department advised Hollywood producers not to condone racial prejudice while America was fighting Germany and Japan. Overnight, the Japanese and Germans became screen villains, and Indians became allies. As government policy changed in the 1950s, assimilation of Indians into American society began to be reflected on the screen. According to many of these movies, such as *The Searchers* (1956), peaceful assimilation was impossible. In the 1950s and 1960s, movies examined the struggles of people of mixed blood or mixed heritage and the conflict over fitting into neither Native nor white society.

By the 1970s, perhaps as a result of the activist movements of the 1960s, westerns began to attack U.S. Indian policies fiercely. U.S. soldiers were now portrayed as killing and maiming innocent Indians. *Little Big Man* (1971) reflected resentment against U.S. involvement in Vietnam and distrust of the government. Several other movies, including *Soldier Blue* (1970) and *Ulzana's Raid* (1972), were openly critical of the U.S. Army's treatment of American Indians.

During the 1970s, westerns became less popular, and Indians in movies began to appear "outside" society's boundaries. *One Flew over the Cuckoo's Nest* (1975) features an Indian character played by Will Sampson confined in a mental institution. In *Harry and Tonto* (1974), Squamish actor Dan George finds himself in a jail cell with an adventurous old man.

Kevin Costner's *Dances with Wolves* (1990) sparked renewed interest in movies with Indian themes. This popular movie cast many Indian actors and portrayed Indians sympathetically. Also, authentic Native languages were used. However, *Dances with Wolves* did little to promote understanding of Native culture. Instead it projects a romantic image of the noble savage. In spite of its popularity, *Dances with Wolves* brought little change to Hollywood's portrayal of Indian life and people.

In 1992, *The Last of the Mohicans* simply reworked an old theme. Hawkeye, a colonial backwoodsman, aided by his faithful Indian companions defeats the Huron leader, Magua. *The Last of the Mohicans* has been filmed at least a dozen times, and was the subject of a television series in 1957-58. The popularity of this story suggests that Hollywood (and perhaps Americans) prefer to isolate Indians safely in the past rather than take a close look at Native American issues today.

Considering the strong role of women in many Native communities, it is not surprising that many Indian playwrights are women. In early European plays, the Native female was often presented as a "gentle native" who offered protection to non-Natives and, in the process, admitted her inferiority. Native women playwrights have worked to dispel such harmful myths while addressing important problems. For example, Spiderwomen Theater in New York is an innovative all-female company whose plays emphasize social issues that affect Native women.

Since the early 1970s, independent filmmakers throughout North America have been creating alternatives to Hollywood films. Independent Indian filmmakers produce movies with their own perspective. *Return of the Country* (1982) is a good example. This film, made by Bob Hicks, a Creek-Seminole, turns the non-Indian perspective on its ear. *In Return of the Country,* Indians discover America and promptly establish a Bureau of Caucasian Affairs (mimicking the real-life Bureau of Indian Affairs). Non-Indian children are forced to abandon the English language, shed their European-style dress, and shun the Christian religion.

A recent Public Broadcasting Service television special, *Surviving Columbus* (1992), traced Pueblo history from European contact to the present. It was written and produced by an all-Indian crew.

Canada's media have encouraged the growth of independent filmmaking among Native peoples in recent years. The National Film Board and Telefilm Canada provide Native filmmakers with funding and distribution. In 1990, the National Film Board created Studio One, which provides training and production assistance to Native filmmakers. Studio One also places Native people in control of Native media messages.

24

Activism

Native Peoples

Protest Loss of Lands and Rights

FACT FOCUS

- Native Americans claimed Alcatraz Island as their own and occupied the empty prison there for almost two years. They were protesting and publicizing the loss of their lands as well as attempting to create a Native American cultural and educational center.
- The Navajo Community College, founded in 1968, was the first tribal college.
- More than one million people in Canada are aboriginal. They belong to 596 different bands (the Canadian term for tribes).
- It was illegal for status Indians in Canada to raise money to form political groups until 1953.

Activism in the United States

American Indian protest started at the beginning of contact with Europeans. In the five hundred years since colonists arrived on their continent, Native North Americans have struggled in a variety of ways to survive and to stand up for rights that were being taken away from them. In the 1700s and 1800s they fought in the battlefields. Later they fought in the courts, on reservations, and on city streets. With their five hundred-year struggle against European-American rule, Native Americans have a long history of political activism (group actions that are aimed at a goal or the solution of a problem).

Native Americans in the United States have a unique legal status that is unlike any other group of people in America. Under the terms of more than four hundred treaties that they hold with the U.S. government, American Indian tribes hold the status of sovereign (self-governing) nations. This means that they have the authority to make and enforce their own laws on the reservations. But Native Americans are also governed by the state, local, and federal laws that govern all Americans. Often local laws conflict with tribal laws. When this occurs, it usually takes a court ruling to decide which authority—the tribe or the local government—has the power to interpret and apply the law on the reservation.

Most Native American activism centers around loss of lands and tribal rights. Some of the rights Indians have fought for include fishing and hunting rights, the right to develop and manage reservation resources, and the right to govern themselves. They have also struggled for the return of sacred objects, grave sites, artwork, and cultural items.

Early Native American Activism

American Indian activism between 1500 and 1800 was primarily fought on battlefields during wars and in smaller skirmishes at other times. When military defeat was undeniable, another important kind of tribal activism, the **revitalization** movement, assured many Native people that spiritual defeat need not follow. Revitalization (or rebirth) movements sought a return to life as it was before Europeans came to settle in North America. One revitalization movement, the Handsome Lake movement, began in 1799 among the Seneca and other Iroquois tribes. Led by a Seneca prophet named Handsome Lake, the movement stressed maintaining Native American traditions within families and tribes and in the way that people used the land. Because the Handsome Lake movement did not totally reject U.S. culture and rule, the government did not take strong action against it.

The Ghost Dance movement, which began in 1869, involved a number of Great Basin and West Coast tribes and, later, Plains

WORDS TO KNOW

aboriginal: native to the land or being the first known inhabitants of an area. In Canada, the word *aboriginal* is often used to replace terms such as "Native American" or "Indian." Both of these terms have been criticized by Native Americans.

Red Power: A term used to describe the Native American activism movement of the 1960s, in which people from many tribes came together to protest the injustices of American policies toward Native Americans.

revitalization: the feeling or movement in which something seems to come back to life after having been quiet or inactive for a period of time.

self-determination: *Self-determination* often means a person's right to choose his or her own way of life. In this chapter, the term refers to the right of a group of people to choose and direct the way of life within their community, including the authority to make and enforce laws.

peoples. The Ghost Dance movement was more radical than the Handsome Lake movement and involved a greater number of people. Members of this movement blamed white people for the miserable state of affairs on reservations and the destruction of Indian ways of life. They predicted the disappearance of white settlers and a return to traditional Native lifestyles.

Unfortunately, the American government

The Quaker City banquet of the Society of American Indians, Hotel Walton, 1914.

did not always respond kindly to these movements. The U.S. military, which viewed the Ghost Dance movement as a threat to national security, often used force to stop Native Americans from openly participating in it. The most infamous example of this kind of military action is the massacre of 370 Indian men, women, and children at Wounded Knee, South Dakota, in 1890. The Ghost Dance movement ended in the early 1890s as the American Indian population was confined to reservations.

American Indian Protest, 1900-1960

In the early 1900s, tribes struggled to survive on reservations without sufficient food or money and far from other tribes or centers of power. There was little energy or funding for Indian protest. Some organizations acted on behalf of Native Americans during this time. The Women's National Indian Association, founded in 1879, and the Indian Rights Association, founded in Philadelphia by Quakers and other Christian reformers in 1882, are the oldest non-Indian groups formed to help Native Americans in the United States. The Indian Rights Association is the oldest group of its kind that is still active today in the United States.

These groups, and a number of others that followed, wanted to preserve Indian cultures and improve living conditions. Although they helped Native Americans, their goals in certain areas differed from the wishes of some of the tribes with whom they worked. One of the goals of these early organizations was to help Indians blend into mainstream American society. As the revitalization movements demonstrate, many Indians sought to preserve their own way of life and did not wish to blend into U.S. culture.

Activism reappeared with the founding of the Indian Defense League of America (IDLA) in the 1920s. The IDLA protested the disregard shown by the American and Canadian governments for Native treaty rights. IDLA protests included refusing to pay customs duties, refusing to use passports, and resisting restrictions on movement between Canada and the United States.

The U.S. government's passage of the Indian Reorganization Act of 1934, which returned some land and granted **sovereignty** (self-rule) to Native American groups, sparked activity on the reservations. Because the government provided more money to the reservations, Native Americans were able to take a new look at their situation and act together to try to correct it. Tribes had to decide whether or not to support the act, which brought land, money, and certain rights, but also brought some questionable new programs to reservations. During this time, the government's Bureau of Indian Affairs interfered with self-government on several reservations and became a target of tribal protest.

After World War II, Indian advocacy groups changed. Their members tended to be only Indian, or mostly Indian, and they focused on tribal rights and **self-determination.** One reason for this change was that

WORDS TO KNOW

sovereignty: self-rule; freedom from the rule or control of outside parties.

status Indians: aboriginal Canadians who are registered with the government as Indians and are therefore entitled to the special benefits due to aboriginals by treaty or by acts of the Canadian government.

wampum belt: Wampum was a Native American word for the beads made of polished shells that many Indian tribes used as money. Wampum was strung on belts or sashes. It served not only as money, but also for decoration.

Native American veterans who returned from the war viewed the reservations and their place in American society in a new light. After fighting and risking their lives on an equal footing with the rest of American society, they began to feel more entitled to society's rewards. The National Congress of American Indians (NCAI) was formed in 1944 by members of many tribes.

Indian activism in the years after World War II was aimed mainly at projects that threatened Indian lands and sacred areas. The Iroquois resisted several water projects that affected their lands. These included Mohawk and Tuscarora protests against the St. Lawrence Seaway project in New York in the 1950s and 1960s. During this period, the Iroquois protested treaty violations each year by demonstrating at the United Nations in New York. They wore traditional cere-

Tuscarora protesting reservoir.

monial clothing and used the media to capture public interest in their cause.

Native American Activism in the 1960s

In the 1960s, the Civil Rights movement sparked widespread reform in the United States. Native American communities responded to the national movement with increased activism. The National Indian Youth Council (NIYC), established in 1961, was concerned with Native American issues both on and off the reservations. The American Indian Movement (AIM) was founded in Minneapolis in 1968. These two groups formed a backbone of Indian activism.

In December 1960, a group of Ute Indians in Utah seceded (withdrew) from the United States in protest of government control over their land and mineral holdings. Although the Utes did not succeed in forming a separate nation, they did succeed in drawing public attention to their cause.

Dozens of American Indian newspapers and magazines were begun in the late 1960s and 1970s. American Indian Studies centers were created at a number of universities. In

Indian students march during "American Indian Heritage Month."

1968 Navajo Community College was founded as the first tribal college. During the next ten years, nearly two dozen community colleges were established on reservations.

Additional organizations were formed, including the National Indian Education Association (1961), the Native American Rights Fund (1970), the National Tribal Chairman's Association (1971), and the Council of Energy Resource Tribes (1975). These groups provided a voice for Native American communities at all levels of government.

The increasing numbers of Indians living in American cities contributed to the growth of Indian activism. During the 1960s the **Red Power** movement—a combination of the efforts of many Native American groups—came to life. The Red Power movement was the term used to describe and include many varieties of Native American activism.

The Fish-ins of the 1960s

In the Civil Rights movement of the 1960s "sit-ins" were a popular form of protest against racist practices such as the refusal of restaurants to serve black Americans at the same counters as white Americans. Native American activism used "fish-

The 1960s and 1970s were a time of Indian protest and, as the courts began to restore treaty rights, some communities took their own initiative in challenging tribal claims in matters like fishing rights.

ins" to protest the loss of their fishing rights in the Northwest.

In a 1957 Supreme Court case in Washington state, Robert Satiacum, a Native American, was tried for fishing out of season. Native Americans held that they were given the right to fish by treaty, and that the state of Washington had no power to determine the season for their fishing. The court's decision was split 4-4, but police continued to restrict fishing activities. And the Indian fishermen continued to cast their nets. National figures like comedian Dick Gregory and actor Marlon Brando supported the fishermen and brought national attention to

the tribes' cause. Finally in 1974 the Indian fishing rights were restored, and the fish-in movement ended. The victory encouraged Red Power activists all over the country to continue their fight to regain their rights.

The Occupation of Alcatraz Island, 1969-71

In the early morning hours of November 20, 1969, 89 Native Americans landed on Alcatraz Island in the San Francisco Bay. Alcatraz was formerly a U.S. penitentiary. The group, calling itself "Indians of All Tribes," claimed possession of the island by the "right of discovery." It justified its actions with an 1868 Sioux Treaty that gave Indians the right to unused federal property on Indian land. The Indians of All Tribes planned to use the island as a center for Native American spiritual, educational, and cultural activity. Part of the statement the Indians of All Tribes gave to the press stated:

> We, the native Americans, re-claim the land known as Alcatraz Island in the name of all American Indians by right of discovery.... We will purchase said Alcatraz for twenty-four dollars in glass beads and red cloth.... Our offer of 1.24 per acre is greater than the 47 cents per acre the white men are now paying the California Indians for their land.

Native Americans, numbering anywhere from 15 to 1,000, occupied Alcatraz for the next 19 months. Usually there were about 100 Native Americans on the island at a time. They came from many different tribes, including the Sioux, Navajo, Cherokee, Mohawk, Puyallup, Yakima, Hoopa, and Omaha. During the months of occupation

Alcatraz Island declaration by Indians of All Tribes.

Powwow singers, Alcatraz Island.

the Indians held news conferences, pow-wows, and celebrations while they negotiated with federal officials. Those occupying Alcatraz had to deal with hardships as federal officials interfered with boats bringing in supplies and cut off the supply of water and electricity to the island. The occupation was very peaceful and the Indians made the American public aware of their position. However, the government did not accept the Indians' offer to purchase the island.

Red Power Takes Native America into the 1970s

Although the protest on Alcatraz did not result in the cultural center that the Indians wanted, Alcatraz provided a clear plan of

action for the Red Power movement that was carried out in other protests. After Alcatraz, the Indians of All Tribes occupied an abandoned Nike missile base in California and later carried out several other actions involving unused federal property. Most of the occupations were peaceful and festive celebrations of Native culture and traditions.

As the 1970s went on, however, the demonstrations took on a more serious and sometimes violent tone. In 1973 a ten-week-long siege at the Pine Ridge reservation came to be known as "Wounded Knee II." Wounded Knee II involved a dispute over the tribal chairman, Richard Wilson. Some tribe members felt Wilson was a puppet of the Bureau of Indian Affairs and wanted to impeach him. Wilson's supporters and opponents armed themselves and began a siege that lasted ten weeks. Federal law enforcement officials, the Bureau of Indian Affairs, local citizens, celebrities, and the national news media all became involved.

The last major event of the Red Power movement occurred in July 1978. Several hundred Native Americans marched into Washington, D.C., at the end of "The Longest Walk." The Longest Walk was a protest that had started in San Francisco five months earlier. It was intended to symbolize the forced removal of Native Americans from their homelands over the past centuries and to draw attention to their continuing problems. The Longest Walk was a peaceful and spiritual event that ended without violence.

As the Red Power movement declined, the federal government reviewed its policies toward Indians in a new light. Government officials were more than aware of Red Power actions and the changes in public

Indians participate in the Longest Walk, a protest to bring attention to broken treaties and ill treatment of Indian people, 1978.

opinion that resulted. Several laws were passed that supported the rights of Native Americans to govern themselves. In 1971 an act was passed recognizing the land rights of the Native people of Alaska and providing them with money and transfers of land. In 1974 a fund was established to give loans to reservations for economic development. Many decision-making rights were transferred from the Bureau of Indian Affairs to the tribes.

The 1980s: Activism in the Courts

During the 1980s, Indian activism shifted its focus from public demonstration to court action. The number of American Indian lawyers increased greatly, and Native Americans increasingly used the legal system to fight for their rights. Three main goals were targeted:

1) Land claims. Many tribes are fighting to have land they legally own returned to them. Some, such as the Passamaquoddy of Maine, have gained from these efforts. They received a multimillion-dollar settlement and have used the money to improve their community. The Passamaquoddy have built a firm to manufacture housing, a timber mill, and other enterprises. Not

all land disputes have been so successful, however.

2) The return of Indian artifacts. Explorers and settlers have always helped themselves to Indian artwork, sacred objects, and other cultural pieces. They have dug up ancient and contemporary Indian grave sites as well. During the 1980s many of the items the Indians wanted returned were given back. For example, in 1989 the Smithsonian Institution returned the skeletal remains and burial artifacts of hundreds of Indians to their modern descendants. The state of New York returned 12 **wampum belts**—held since the late 1800s—to the Onondaga Nation. The Onondaga Nation had been trying to get these back for over 30 years.

3) The right of tribes to govern themselves. Many Native American tribes fought for control of water rights, hunting and fishing rights, and mineral and resource rights. They sought religious freedoms and the right to develop manufacturing, tourism, recreation, and other businesses on the reservations. Gambling parlors on reservations have remained a controversial issue in some areas. Many of these battles continue today.

Canadian Activism

Since the 1960s, **aboriginal** (Native) peoples in Canada have formed a number of groups to represent their interests to the government and to the Canadian people as well. Some of these groups focus on particular issues, such as women's rights. Other organizations were formed to provide ser-

vices to aboriginals, such as policing or child protection.

Canadian organizations

Over one million people in Canada are aboriginal. Four nationwide political organizations and at least three aboriginal women's groups form an important structure used by Native Canadians to address their issues to the nation.

The Assembly of First Nations represents **status Indians** in Canada. A status Indian is an aboriginal registered with the government and is entitled to certain special benefits. The Assembly of First Nations represents about 700,000 people. Two-thirds of these people live on reserves (reservations). Members come from all 596 Canadian bands (tribes). When the government needs to consult status Indians, the Assembly of First Nations is the group they most often turn to.

The Native Council of Canada (NCC) was formed originally to represent all aboriginal people who were neither status Indians nor Inuit. This group of people is very large, probably larger than the status Indian group. Their concerns and interests are very different since they live in cities rather than on reserves.

In 1983 some of the NCC members left to form a new group, the Métis National Council. This group is based in the western provinces of Alberta, Saskatchewan, Manitoba, and the Northwest Territories. They are descendants of the Red River Métis who emerged in the late 1700s and early 1800s. The Métis (meaning "mixed") descend from unions between French and Scottish fur traders and aboriginal people. The Red River Métis developed their own distinct culture, with its own language and sense of identity. In the 1800s this group fought against the colonial leaders of Canada for their right to self-govern. Led in their battles by dedicated and valiant leaders such as Louis Riel and Gabriel Dumont, the Métis established a tradition of democracy that unites them even today.

The fourth nationwide aboriginal group is the Inuit Tapirisat of Canada. This body represents the Canadian Inuit (formerly called Eskimos), whose homeland is the vast Arctic region of Canada. The Arctic covers about one-third of Canada, and in most areas where the Inuit live, they are the majority. The Inuit Tapirisat represents all Inuit, regardless of where they live.

There are three main aboriginal organizations for women in Canada. Inuit women formed Pauktuutit, which represents all Inuit women in Canada. The Native Women's Association of Canada represents mainly status Indian women, and Métis women have formed the Women of the Métis Nation.

History of the Organizations

The conflict between the aboriginal peoples and foreign settlers in Canada is at least 450 years old. Yet all the existing political organizations for aboriginal peoples were formed in the late 1960s and early 1970s. There are several reasons that aboriginal groups did not organize sooner:

1) Until 1953 it was illegal for status Indians in Canada to raise funds to form political groups. Until 1959 status Indians could not vote in the Parliament.

2) Federal officials supervised Indian bands closely, giving them few opportunities to organize.

3) Many aboriginals were poor and did not have the resources to organize, especially over the large geographical areas they inhabited.

4) Some groups, such as the Inuit and Métis, lived in areas that had attracted few outsiders or industrial activities. These Indians were able to live their lives more or less as they wished and saw little need for political activity.

From 1921 to the mid-1970s, no treaties were signed in Canada between aboriginals and the government, although large portions of the country still were not covered by treaty. But after World War II a new awareness of civil rights emerged in Canada and by the 1970s treaty-making began again. The treaties were called "comprehensive claims agreements." Eventually aboriginal groups received funding to represent their interests.

The economy changed after World War II. Developments of mines, hydroelectric projects, and oil and gas exploration brought many outsiders to northern Canada. Now there was competition for the land that aboriginals had been using for harvesting food and furs.

The Canadian government, by not treating Indians fairly, also brought on Canadian Indian activism. A 1969 government study, called a White Paper, reported that status Indians did have certain rights as a result of treaties they had signed. Soon after this, a new government was elected, which issued a new White Paper. The new government proposed to end all special rights for aboriginals in Canada and to take strong actions to help the aboriginals blend into the rest of society.

This 1969 White Paper led to immediate protest. The government changed its position quickly, but the aboriginal groups had already taken up a course of activism. The government responded by creating a policy to settle land claims. They proposed to give aboriginals money and other benefits, if the aboriginals would give up all rights to the land forever.

By 1993 four comprehensive claims had been settled, but many more are still being negotiated. Many aboriginal groups will not accept the idea of giving up their lands forever. To them it is as unthinkable as giving up their civil rights. Aboriginals want their political rights stated clearly, and the government is not eager to do this.

Some groups are looking for new solutions to these age-old problems with the government. One such solution has been the formation of a new territory in Canada. Nunavit will not be a reserve or reservation, but a new area that may someday become a province. Here the Inuit will probably form a large majority of the population for many years. This will give them considerable political power. Nunavit will end the Inuit land claim by giving the Inuit rights to small plots of land in the territory.

The aboriginal political groups now have many of the responsibilities for governing their peoples. New organizations provide a way for aboriginal people to struggle against poverty and racism and to build a better future. Canadian Indian struggles have already created a growing understanding among Canadians of the aboriginals' needs for services and political activity.

INDEX